ADDRESSING
SYSTEMIC DISCRIMINATION
BY
REFRAMING THE
PROBLEM

Dr. Frank L. Douglas

Published by Frank Douglas Books

Addressing Systemic Discrimination By Reframing The Problem

ACKNOWLEDGEMENTS

I want to thank our Victors over Injustice in their Professions (VIP) for their discussions on the issues of Equity, Inclusion, and A Better Problem to Solve. VIP members included:

Aubrey Bentham, Ph.D.
Katrina Douglas
Sandra C. Haynes, M.D.
Reginald Jennings J.D.
Frank D. LaSaracina CPA
Judith Lee CPA
Bernice Lowe Flowers
Levern McElveen MPA
Valencia Sanders
Leticia Toledo-Sherman Ph.D.

Thanks to Christina Dose for her assistance with the graphics.

Special thanks to:

Bernice Lowe, Sandra Haynes, and Levern McElveen for identifying most of the interviewees whose cases were selected for presentation.

Frank LaSaracina for his support with graphic representations and assignment of microaggressions.

Dr. Sandra Haynes for serving as a discussant partner and for performing initial editing.

TABLE OF CONTENTS

**SAFE HAVEN DIALOGUES' REFRAMING PROCESS
PART ONE**

**SAFE HAVEN DIALOGUES' REFRAMING PROCESS
PART TWO**

INTRODUCTION

The present primer was motivated by two events. The first event was the sight of the murder of George Floyd and being horrified that, despite desperate pleas, sympathetic onlookers could not get Chauvin to take his knee off George Floyd's neck. The stark reality was that only one individual was being murdered - George Floyd.

The second event was my subsequent reflection on cases of racism with which I have been involved. In every case, there was an individual who was significantly harmed. This train of thought evolved to my reflections on the efforts in Diversity, Equity, and Inclusion (DEI).

Many of these programs stress recruiting and retaining individuals of diverse demographics and sensitizing organizations to issues, such as **microaggressions**, that adversely impact Inclusion. However, in many cases, the Aggrieved Individuals do not benefit directly from these programs. For example, despite the presence of these programs, 33% of Black employees don't feel respected or valued at work (1).

Two factors seemed to be missing. The first is that the Aggrieved did not feel they were being heard. Their complaints were not heard and their pain was not felt. Second, their supervisors and colleagues demonstrated little empathy. This led to the creation of Safe Haven Dialogues LLC.

The goal of Safe Haven Dialogues (SHD) is to empower the Aggrieved Individual to have a dialogue with their supervisor in order to find a solution that would increase the productivity of both the Aggrieved as well as the department in which they work.

This primer describes and applies the SHD Reframing Process to real cases. These cases are based on interviews in which the names of the individuals and their organizations have been altered to preserve their anonymity. The SHD panel evaluated each case using the Reframing Process and documented the key issues of Equity and Inclusion. They then explored ways to Reframe the Problem by finding a Better Problem to Solve.

It is our hope that this primer will provide groups the opportunity to discuss each case and similarly implement the Reframing Process to find productive solutions for both the Aggrieved and their organization.

The intent is not to suggest that the solutions recorded in this primer are the only practical ones. Rather, it is hoped that groups will identify instances which are similar to one or more of these cases; 'walk in the shoes' of the Aggrieved; and apply the SHD Reframing Process to find impactful solutions for cases of Systemic Discrimination.

We also believe that the SHD Reframing Process can be extrapolated to solving other problems, particularly if there are components of deeply held opposing views.

SAFE HAVEN DIALOGUES' REFRAMING PROCESS

PART ONE

ADDRESSING
SYSTEMIC DISCRIMINATION

MAKING IT PERSONAL
BY
REFRAMING THE PROBLEM
AT THE

Equity and Inclusion Intersection

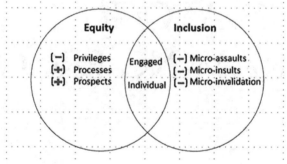

Chapter 1

EQUITY, INCLUSION, AND INDIVIDUAL ENGAGEMENT

Focus on Equity and Inclusion

This Primer is based on the construct that, while human beings prefer simple solutions, the discomfort of having difficult conversations leads to avoidance or unnecessary complexity. Nonetheless, our better selves know the following with certainty: no one likes to be told that they do not belong, no one likes to be treated unfairly, and no one likes to be robbed of the motivation and the joy of contributing. Everyone likes to feel valued. As a result, the most difficult issues in the social aspects of life can be viewed simply from two principles: Equity and Inclusion. For example, what decision would the Supreme Court of the United States of America have made if they had looked at the Dobbs case (Roe vs. Wade) from the perspectives of Equity and Inclusion, as opposed to Pro-Life vs. Pro-Choice?

The Equity perspective would have addressed the unfairness of selectively punishing women by taking away their right to make a decision about their lives, while not holding the men who helped create the dilemma to account. The debate over Inclusion might have caused them to reflect on the unexpected consequences for a child victim of rape or for a mother with a nonviable pregnancy, who had been deprived of the right to make life-changing decisions.

Discrimination is not new. It has been practiced for centuries, with deadly consequences, by both religious and governmental entities. Each professed a creed that actually paid little attention to Equity or Inclusion.

Another difficult problem that this primer addresses is the reluctance to 'walk a mile in someone else's shoes.' This is a simple yet often eschewed way to understand what those who have lived a different reality feel. Here is a personal example.

I recently reached out to a former colleague for help extracting examples of **microaggressions** *from the minutes of interviews that form the basis of the Reframing Process in this Primer. My colleague, a White female, began to express her frustrations that Black men try to flee when confronted by police and end up being killed.*
'They must have done something wrong. Otherwise, why would they run,' she mused.
I responded, "Let me tell you of a situation I experienced five years ago, at the age 74.

It was about 9 pm, and I was returning from a dinner meeting with a colleague. I live in an upscale, oceanfront, gated condominium complex with about a 150-foot walk to the beach. Through the gate, I saw three Police cars near my parking spot. I drove slowly into my parking spot, and the three police cars closed in behind me as if to block any attempt I might make to escape.

I thought it strange as I could not see anyone else as I entered the condominium complex. Two policemen approached me, one on either side of my car, and motioned for me to open my window. I complied.
The one closest to me said, 'you left the scene of an accident.'
I responded, 'I was not involved in an accident. In fact, I am just returning from dinner at a restaurant about 3-4 miles from here.'
'Get out of the car,' he demanded.

I opened the door slowly, stepped out of the car, and looked up at the windows of the condominium complex to see if any of my neighbors were observing this interaction. My heart sank, and my fear began to rise as I saw no shadows or faces in the windows. It was clear, that since the police officers knew where I lived, they had checked my license plate. This means that it was highly likely they knew who I was. They were also aware, based on their background check, that I had no criminal record nor outstanding traffic tickets. The fact that I was a physician-scientist and CEO of a small Biotech company made no difference.

'Step away from the car,' he ordered.
I took two steps away from the car and away from him. Two of the other police officers were examining the surface of the back bumper and trunk of my car with large flashlights. They illuminated the areas of interest and ran their hands on my vehicle.
Suddenly one said, 'See, here is a smudge!'
I explained that I had the car treated to protect it from the sand, and it had not yet thoroughly dried. I further suggested that they would have the same result if they ran their hands on other parts of the car.
One of the other cops ran his hand on the door as he shone his light on it and produced the same result.
They huddled. After a brief discussion, one of them said, 'seems like it was an error.' They then got into their cars and left."

To my surprise, my colleague airily said: 'Oh, it was probably just a mistake.'
I explained that I was particularly scared since I could not see any potential witnesses observing the event. My colleague persisted in her view that it was probably a mistake. Finally, I responded: 'Do you think that, if I were White and had been suspected of having had a minor accident, **SIX** *police officers would have been waiting for me at my residence? Would they have on finding a smudge, declared it as proof that I was involved in an accident? Would they have departed without an apology? Can you understand the fear that I experienced wondering whether the outcome would have been tragic, given the spate of Black men being killed by police officers for seemingly minor infractions?'*

Silence ensued, and the conversation ended.

As a physician, I know that fear stimulates our body's biological response of Fight-or-Flight. It is the feeling every Black man in America experiences when confronted by a show of force from the police, whether they have committed a crime or not. In my case, the show of force was unnecessary, and the instinct to succumb to flight was triggered.

In that moment, I was no exception. However, my greater surprise was that although my colleague knew me well, nonetheless, she could not take a **walk in my shoes** that night! She did not, would not, or could not empathize with my fear! This is the phenomenal tragedy of Systemic Discrimination. It is not that good people do nothing. It is that good people feel nothing!

The large percentage of Black, Indigenous, and People of Color (BIPOC) who are killed by police has led researchers to call this a 'public health emergency.' (Journal of Epidemiology and Community Health). Unarmed Black people are killed by police at three times the rate of White people. The public, callous murder of George Floyd almost appears to be a natural outcome of the facts in the first two sentences of this paragraph. It awakened the conscience and consciousness of the nation to the reality of Systemic Discrimination.

In the aftermath, more CEOs joined the initial 700 who signed the CEO Action for Diversity and Inclusion™. The initiative was organized in 2017 with the aim of 'rallying the business community to advance diversity and inclusion within the workplace.' Yet, according to the Society of Human Resource Management (SHRM), 33 % of Black employees in companies with DEI programs feel like outsiders (1).

In our view, despite the excellent work being done on DEI, two essential variables are frequently missing. These are resolute commitment to Equity and a palpable passion for Inclusion. Diversity reflects metrics that quantify the different types of individuals or ideas. Inclusion focuses on Individuals and their meaningful participation. Equity represents the foundational processes that signal to individuals within the organization that they are valued.

SHD considers that both Equity and Inclusion are necessary to address Systemic Discrimination effectively. Leaders need to ensure that there is Equity for **everyone** in the organization. We have observed that, when members of the majority group do not feel they are being treated equitably, they have no capacity to feel empathy, and hence cannot discuss Equity for their marginalized colleagues.

Reviewing rules and regulations are important in assessing the efficacy of Equity. We recommend three dimensions from which to evaluate rules and regulations. These dimensions are: **Privilege/Preferences, Processes, and Prospects**. Privilege/Preferences refers to employees with special status. Processes refer to the way rules and policies are administered. Prospects pertain to opportunities for development, advancement, and retention in the organization.

In hierarchical as well as relatively flat organizations, individuals with preferential status and various concomitant privileges can emerge. These individuals are often easily identified by the preferred assignments they receive, their visibility to leaders, their visibility within the organization, and the lack of severe criticism for poor performance. Preferred/Privileged individuals benefit from the flexibility in the implementation of Processes, and their Prospects remain bright. A critical examination of these three dimensions, aids in identifying whether the culture is equitable or unfair.

Examples of critical questions to be asked are:

- Do the rules and regulations permit Privilege or Preference for some groups?
- Are Processes applied identically, without exceptions, to everyone?
- Are the Prospects of each individual transparent and related to their performances and contributions to the organization's mission and goals?

Inclusion can be elusive, and there are many strategies to encourage it. However, when a marginalized individual is not included, they feel it profoundly. In fact, exclusion as a concept and a reality is easier to describe than inclusion. Interestingly, although an individual might remain sanguine when faced with inequities in a system, the reaction is instinctive when that individual is faced with a lack of inclusion. This is not subtle and can be recognized by the presence of **microaggressions**. **Microaggressions** are experienced personally and identifying incidences of **Microassaults, Microinsults, and Microinvalidations** is one way to assess whether an individual is in a culture that does not support behaviors that embrace Inclusion.

We specifically look at some of the negative practices connected with denying Inclusion because these are powerfully experienced and easy to demonstrate when they occur.

- **Microassaults** refer to actions and words, such as slurs and racial epithets, that are intended to demean an individual.
- **Microinsults** are the verbal and non-verbal actions that are used as stereotypes that degrade one's identity, such as one's gender or ethnicity.
- **Microinvalidations** are actions or communications intended to subtly or openly weaken and even negate the legitimacy of someone's status, achievements, or contributions.

It should be noted that a verbal or non-verbal action could fit more than one type of **microaggression.** For example, if a professor accuses a Black student of malingering, and after discovering that he had misjudged the student, says, 'well, that's what your type usually does.' This is both a **microassault** and a **microinsult.** It is a **microassault** because he demeaned the student directly, and it is a **microinsult** because he lowered the student's status by applying a stereotype to the student's ethnicity.

Equity, Inclusion, Individual Engagement Principle – EIIEP

Studies have shown a significant and bidirectional relationship between job and life satisfaction. Individuals spend about 12 hours a day preparing for work, at work, and traveling to and from work. Hence, on average, an individual spends 50% of their awake time on work-related activities that support their Life, Liberty, and the Pursuit of Happiness. Thus, given the relationship between job satisfaction and life satisfaction, it is certainly important to provide job satisfaction for employees. It turns out that providing job satisfaction to employees is also important for the company.

In its 2020 report, Gallup published the results of its large-scale study spanning 112,000 teams, including 2.7 million workers in 276 organizations across 54 industries in 96 countries, for three decades. They concluded that Employee Engagement contributed to:

- 81% lower absenteeism,
- 64% fewer safety incidents (accidents),
- 23% higher profitability,
- 66% higher well-being (net thriving employees)

When comparing median percent differences in top-quartile and bottom-quartile engagement in business/work units, Gallup concluded: 'The relationship between engagement and performance at the business/work unit level continues to be substantial and highly generalizable across companies' (2). In fact, several companies, including Nationwide and Roche, are focusing on Employee Engagement as a critical business strategy while some DEI programs include Employee Engagement content in their materials.

Diversity has traditionally been the foundation of Diversity, Equity, and Inclusion (DEI). It was considered morally important to include employees from diverse backgrounds, and the contribution of varied ideas to innovative research and marketing provided the business rationale. The discipline progressed, from Diversity (D) to Diversity and Inclusion (D&I), as practitioners began to recognize that, if Diverse individuals are not effectively included in the operations and decision-making processes, the benefits of Diversity are not realized.

Most recently, the critical role of Equity has been recognized, and this led to DEI. Safe Haven Dialogues (SHD) LLC has concluded that if one starts with 'the end in mind', which is the productivity of the organization, a different focus is needed.

Individual Engagement contributes powerfully to this end. Productivity is driven by two variables: the organization's strategy or goals and the commitment of every employee to realizing those goals.

The organization's senior leaders establish the goals and the overall culture via rules and regulations. This forms the basis of Equity for the entire organization. The managers and supervisors of the various departments are responsible for the subcultures, where behaviors that foster productivity are developed and reinforced. This is the basis of Inclusion, without which, Individual Engagement and resulting productivity and profitability do not occur.

The reality of these relationships led me to create the **Equity, Inclusion, and Individual Engagement Principle (EIIEP)** to achieve two goals. One is to contribute to the overall business health of the organization, and second is the empowerment of every Individual in the organization to pursue Life, Liberty, and Happiness.

Diversity, be it gender, sexual orientation, culture, or ideas, emanates from the physical and essential characteristics of the Individual. Since there is no question about the contribution of diversity to innovation, the focus must be on Individuals and on aligning Equity and Inclusion to optimize Individual Engagement.

Equity + Inclusion = Individual Engagement

As previously asserted, Equity specifies and implements the policies and rules that establish the organization's culture and values. This is the responsibility of the senior leaders. Effective implementation of the rules and policies of Equity is necessary but not sufficient to create Individual Engagement. Equity must work with Inclusion to produce the desired goal of increased productivity through the contributions of Engaged Individuals. Whereas Equity has to do with the organization's rules and policies, Inclusion comprises the behaviors, as practiced by managers, supervisors, and co-workers, that integrate every member and their contributions into the department.

Equity and Inclusion work together to create the Culture in which Individual Engagement can flourish. This reality requires a department manager to alert senior managers when Equity and Inclusion are in conflict or are not mutually supportive. A common example of this is when Privilege is present in the company. **In our view, Equity is the Constitution, and Inclusion is 'We the people.'**

In short, Inclusion without Equity can be a Delusion.

Equity and Inclusion are essential principles, without which there can be no genuine nor realistic attempt to eradicate Systemic Discrimination. As stated above, both are necessary. Using one or the other is not sufficient to address the unconscious and conscious behaviors that enable Systemic Discrimination. Indeed, there must be a continual dialogue between the providers of **Equity** and the practitioners of **Inclusion** to reduce significant instances of Systemic Discrimination.

I proffer Individual Engagement, instead of Diversity, as the metric for monitoring whether progress is being made in decreasing Systemic Discrimination. The sad truth is that humans are motivated by productivity and financial gain. 'Because it is the right thing to do' is neither persuasive nor unanimously accepted as 'the right thing to do.'

As mentioned above, the 30-Year Gallup study has been robust in demonstrating that companies with greater than average employee engagement have improved productivity and profitability compared to their peers. This is the current rationale also for committing to social and community improvements.

Equity-Inclusion Culture Matrix

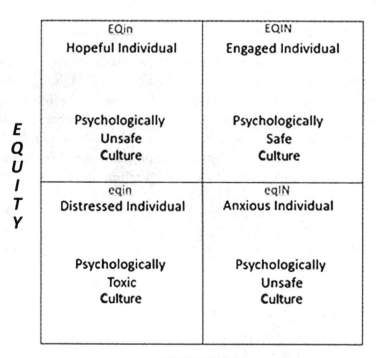

INCLUSION

I designed The Equity – Inclusion Culture Matrix (as shown in the figure above) to demonstrate the dynamics and impact of the interaction between Equity and Inclusion in an organization. Each quadrant or cell can be viewed as the force field within which the Individual exists as they experience both the rules and processes designed by senior leaders and the behaviors of the department as fostered by managers. Each quadrant describes the overall psychological culture created by the interaction between Equity and Inclusion and what the Individual experiences.

In a Psychologically Safe Culture (**EQIN**), both Equity and Inclusion are high. Processes are transparent and are fairly implemented. Privileged groups are discouraged, and every individual can rely on the fact that performance and contributions will determine future prospects in the organization. The manager ensures that behaviors in the department are acceptable and that all team members fully respect the uniqueness of each individual and recognize each other's ideas and contributions. Each individual in this quadrant has the potential to become fully **Engaged** and productive, and this becomes an **EEQIN-Psychologically Safe Culture** for that individual.

In the **HEQin-Psychologically Unsafe Culture**, Equity is high, but Inclusion is low. The individual remains **Hopeful (H)** that senior leaders will remove or positively influence any manager who does not implement the behaviors that support Inclusion. In the case of the **AeqIN-Psychologically Unsafe Culture**, Equity is low and Inclusion is high. The individual remains **Anxious** because they do not know whether or not the Manager who is implementing behaviors that support Inclusion will be removed by the senior leadership for whom Equity is not important. They also know that **Inclusion without Equity can be a Delusion**.

Finally, a **Deqin-Psychologically Toxic Culture**, where both Equity and Inclusion are low, should be avoided at all costs. Unfortunately, such organizations survive because there are many **Distressed** individuals who do not have an alternative. A **Deqin-Psychologically Toxic Culture** is usually characterized by significant turnover.

The goal of every organization should be to become an **EEQIN** organization, as the goal of every individual is to be **fully engaged** in an **EEQIN** organization.

Improvement of Individual Engagement contributes both to the Individual's well-being and the department's productivity. Safe Haven Dialogues' approach expands the evolution of the field from a focus on D (Diversity) through D&I (Diversity & Inclusion), and DEI (Diversity, Equity, and Inclusion) to **EIIEP (Equity, Inclusion, and Individual Engagement Principle).** Equity and Inclusion drive Individual Engagement. The intersections between Equity and Inclusion describe the cultures in which individuals in an organization work.

In the next chapter, we will show you how the Equity – Inclusion Culture Matrix is used to help Aggrieved Individuals find solutions by Reframing the Problem.

Chapter 2

THE SHD REFRAMING PROCESS

Focus on Individual Engagement

In Chapter 1, we introduced the Equity, Inclusion, and Individual Engagement Principle (EIIEP) as the natural evolution of DEI in addressing Systemic Discrimination. We also focused on the critical importance of the interaction between Equity and Inclusion in establishing cultures within an organization that either support or hamper the ability of employees to become fully engaged. In this chapter, we will describe the Reframing Process that Safe Haven Dialogues (SHD) has developed to empower Aggrieved Individuals to deal with Systemic Discrimination and increase their engagement in their work.

Psychologically Unsafe and Toxic Cultures generate reactions that are often under-appreciated. The cases in this primer demonstrate examples of such cultures and offer recommendations on how to improve them and empower individuals to become fully engaged.

The first reaction created by these cultures is '**Loss of Voice**'. Loss of voice occurs at three levels. At the First Level, the Aggrieved Individual feels so defeated that they have lost the will to protest the ill-treatment they are experiencing. At the Second Level, there is no empathetic voice or ally to help the Aggrieved Individual present their case. This aspect of Loss of Voice demonstrates the detrimental effects of the absence of Inclusion in the culture.

Finally, weaknesses in Equity in the culture are contributory factors to Loss of Voice at the Third Level. This occurs when no official processes are readily accessible for the Aggrieved Individual to voice and seek resolution for their pain.

The second reaction, which is positive, is what I call the **Hopeful Plan to Endure the Pain (HPEP)**. This is a situation wherein individuals have a long-term goal or a life necessity that helps them endure the daily pain of inequity and exclusion. One difference between privileged and ordinary individuals is that the Privileged usually have more than one Hopeful Plan to Endure the Pain. Several of the interviewees also described experiencing PTSD-like symptoms from their experience with the continual assault from Systemic Discrimination. It has led us to wonder whether Psychologically Unsafe and Toxic Cultures are producing **Organizational Cultural Stress Disorder (OCSD)** that is seldom recognized and often underestimated.

SHD is convinced that the critical levers in addressing Systemic Discrimination in organizations are Equity and Inclusion. As stated earlier Equity is achieved through fidelity to the rules and regulations created by the senior leaders to ensure fairness in their organizations. Inclusion consists of the behaviors practiced by managers, supervisors, and coworkers. These behaviors ensure that every individual's uniqueness and contributions are valued and included in the daily functioning of their department.

The harmony of Equity and Inclusion creates cultures that enhance the ability of individuals to become engaged and motivated (see Chapter 1). This underscores the importance and relevance of the **Equity, Inclusion, and Individual Engagement Principle**, in which Equity and Inclusion are critical to producing Individual Engagement.

The interaction between Equity and Inclusion determines the types of Cultures in organizations. We represent these in the Equity – Inclusion Culture Matrix and describe the Psychologically Safe Culture, two types of Psychologically Unsafe Cultures, and the Psychologically Toxic Culture. We also describe four types of individuals in these Cultures: Engaged, Hopeful, Anxious, and Distressed.

Misalignment of Equity and Inclusion can be experienced at the departmental level and at the individual level. SHD focuses on the individual, at the micro level, to find the macro levers to address Systemic Discrimination in the organization.

I have developed and implemented our SHD **Reframing Process** to empower the Aggrieved Individuals to address Systemic Discrimination. The SHD Reframing Process has components that include:

1) Giving the Aggrieved an opportunity to be heard;
2) Providing the listener an opportunity to 'walk in the shoes' of the Aggrieved, and thus understand the consequences of a lack of Inclusion;
3) Providing a view of the role that Equity plays in the organization; and
4) Identifying opportunities that can enable the Aggrieved to increase their Engagement in the organization.

Below is a more detailed description of the SHD Reframing Process.

Step 1: Ensure that the Aggrieved is **heard.**

The effect of Loss of Voice is the feeling that one has not been **heard.** SHD has introduced two features that let the Aggrieved know that they are being heard.

The first feature is the SHD Reframe Intake Form. This form is designed to help the Aggrieved describe the problem as cogently as possible by focusing on the key issues. These are the: **DESIRED OUTCOME, SITUATION, ENVIRONMENT, and PROBLEM STATEMENT.** The Form is available via email from SHD.

The Aggrieved is encouraged to be as brief as possible and to use no more than the two pages and allotted spaces on the form. The individual is also encouraged to use bullets of no more than 1-2 sentences to describe each feature of the respective items on the SHD Reframe Intake Form. If requested, SHD will complete the Intake Form via interview and require the Aggrieved to review the written summary of the interview for accuracy.

The second aspect of being heard is the involvement of SHD's **Victors over Injustice in their Professions (VIPs)**. The VIPs are professionals from marginalized communities who have successfully overcome episodes of Discrimination. These individuals have also walked in the shoes of the Aggrieved. In addition, they have been trained in the

SHD Reframing Process to help the Aggrieved find solutions that are productive for both the Aggrieved and the organization.

Step 2: Walk in the shoes of the Aggrieved.

This consists of the following approach: First, the VIP panel (3 members) asks the Aggrieved questions, for clarification only, about the experiences they recorded on the SHD Reframe Intake Form.
Second, based on what was captured on the Form, the VIP identifies instances of **microassaults, microinsults, and microinvalidations**.
In this manner, the VIP panel will be given the opportunity to walk in the shoes of the Aggrieved as they experience the lack of Inclusion in the department.
The VIP members focus on how these **microaggressions** prevent the Aggrieved individual from becoming fully engaged at work. They also discuss what the leader of the department or supervisor could do to change the Situation.

Step 3. Understand the overall culture of the organization with respect to Equity.

Based on the information on the Intake Form, the VIP panel identifies the presence or absence of **Privilege/Preferences**; existence and accessibility of **Processes** that help individuals deal with inequities in the organization; and **Prospects** for the Individual in the organization. Once the VIP members identify possible existence of each of these, they will discuss what the Senior leaders can do to address such problems.

Step 4. Identify solutions for the Aggrieved.

Evaluation of the Equity – Inclusion Culture Matrix.

Based on the outcome of Steps 2 and 3, the VIP panel identifies the quadrant of the Equity – Inclusion Culture Matrix where the Aggrieved presently resides. It is important to determine whether the Aggrieved is Hopeful, Anxious, Distressed, or Engaged.

The VIP panel next explores what is A Better Problem to Solve.

This should have the following characteristics:

Realistic Desired Outcome

It is important to help the Aggrieved individual identify the Desired Outcome that is achievable within the context of the department, preferably with a "hook." It has to be something that will appeal to the management as having a realistic possibility of achieving better results, including higher productivity, greater revenue, lower employee turnover, etc.

Realistic Time Frame

Often the Aggrieved individual has suffered a long time.

On the one hand, the time frame needs to be short enough so that the Aggrieved individual has enough reason to be motivated. However, it also must not be so brief a timeframe that it is unrealistic to expect positive results. A Realistic Time Frame is probably about three months.

Realistic Dialogue between Aggrieved and Manager

No change will occur without this Dialogue. Thus, the Reframing Process should empower the Aggrieved individual to approach the manager and present the topics to be discussed in a manner that recruits the attention, and ultimately, support of the manager.

Realistic for more than the Aggrieved

Often there are other individuals in a department or organization who are experiencing problems similar to those of the Aggrieved. Discussing the issue with these individuals can help identify common pain points and areas, which if improved, could benefit others and increase the engagement of several other stakeholders in an organization.

Realistic Increased Engagement of the Aggrieved and their Department

This is the best goal. If no other members of the department have similar problems, the Aggrieved should focus on their own increased engagement.

A young Black man (YB) was hired by a top fortune 100 company shortly after receiving his Ph.D. in Chemistry from a prestigious university. For three months he could not get assigned to a meaningful project, even after several discussions with his manager. One day a young White man, who was still working on his Ph. D. thesis, was hired and within one week of hire, he was assigned to the 'hottest' project in the R&D department. The Black employee went to his manager to ask when he would be assigned to a meaningful project. After hearing the usual excuses, the Black employee said to his manager: 'think of me as though I were Bob. What project would you assign me? To YB's surprise, his manager became reflective and said: 'yes, you are right. Bob has just joined us, and I have put him on the Drali Project.' The Drali Project was the top project in the department at that time. YB charged out of his manager's office and went to the SVP to recount this most recent example of discrimination against him. Months later, as YB reflected on the incident, he realized that he had overlooked an important fact. The SVP had insisted on the hiring of three Black Ph.Ds. to add to the single Black Ph.D. in the Research & Development department. YB's success was therefore very important to the SVP. Hence, instead of putting the SVP under pressure to deal with the discrimination issue, YB should have asked the SVP to assist his manager in assigning him to a good project. In so doing, he would have given the SVP the space to use his influence with the manager. Ultimately, in this manner, YB would have achieved his Desired Outcome, as that was clearly within the sphere of influence of the SVP. This is the essence of Reframing the Problem to achieve the Desired Outcome. YB would have found a Better Problem to Solve.

After the VIP panel has identified where the Aggrieved is positioned in the Equity- Inclusion Culture Matrix, they then assess which problems are likely to satisfy features of a Better Problem to Solve. A critical feature of selecting a Better Problem is to specifically evaluate the points of influence that can be recruited. This will depend on whether the Aggrieved is presently positioned in an **EQIN**, **EQin**, **eqin**, or an **eqIN** quadrant, where upper case **EQ** and **IN** represent quadrants where Equity and Inclusion are strong, respectively.

Similarly, lower case **eq** and lower case **in**, represent quadrants where Equity and Inclusion are low, respectively. Once the quadrant is selected, the VIP panel reviews the Desired Outcome and Problem Statement to determine whether a solution would meet the criteria of a Better Problem to Solve. If this is not possible, the VIP panel would recommend a different Desired Outcome that would facilitate a solution to the Problem being endured by the Aggrieved.

Thus, the core of the Reframing Process is first to understand which quadrant of the Equity – Inclusion Culture Matrix the Aggrieved Individual occupies. This helps to determine the points of influence in Equity and Inclusion that could be used to Reframe the Problem. It might be quite different from the Culture which other co-workers, for example, those who are privileged, enjoy!

FINDING THE BETTER PROBLEM TO SOLVE

Finding a Better Problem to Solve is the climactic step in the SHD Reframing Process. It comprises the following steps:

A) Review of the Desired Outcome
B) Identification of the quadrant in which the Aggrieved individual resides
C) Identification of the points of influence with respect to voice and allies in Equity and Inclusion that the Aggrieved might have in the quadrant
D) Use of the points of influence to identify opportunities to improve productivity in the department
E) Identification of the opportunities for the Aggrieved to contribute to productivity improvements
F) Identification of the opportunity for the Aggrieved to become engaged

If the individual is in either a High Equity (**EQ**) or a High Inclusion (**IN**) Culture, this is a little easier because this suggests that senior managers or line managers are committed to fostering respectful cultures. However, it should be noted that if Equity is highly positive, it makes it easier to foster Inclusion behaviors that will lead to Engaged Individuals. On the other hand, if Equity is very low in the organization, strong efforts at Inclusion might not succeed in producing Engaged Individuals.

A Better Problem to Solve might be found in any Culture including in a Psychologically Toxic Culture (**eqin**). Sometimes, as in a situation when the Culture is psychologically toxic, the solution for a Better Problem to Solve includes leaving this organization in order to preserve one's well-being. In this instance, the VIP panel would also explore with the Aggrieved Individual potential Hopeful Plans to Endure the Pain.

REFRAMING THE PROBLEM

The final step in the Reframing Process is using the Better Problem to Solve to reframe the Problem and, occasionally, the Desired Outcome. In the anecdote in this chapter, the Desired Outcome would have become: 'Finding a meaningful project that will facilitate my contributions to the unit.'

A Better Problem to Solve would have been to request the SVP to assist the manager in finding a meaningful project for YB. The significance of the involvement of the SVP in solving this problem would not have been lost on the manager.

Once a Better Problem to Solve has been selected, the VIP panel discusses the challenges that the Aggrieved would face in having a Dialogue with their manager. The VIP panel uses this information to identify the Reframed Problem that would effectively engage the appropriate manager.

The rest of this Primer presents examples of cases obtained via interviews, with summaries of the VIP panel's assessment of the aspects of Inclusion, Equity, A Better Problem to Solve, and the Reframed Problem. The intent of the Primer is not only to give tangible examples of the SHD REFRAMING PROCESS but also to encourage groups to use these cases to practice identifying Better Problems to Solve. This will help many to 'walk in the shoes' of others and become motivated to build cultures where Equity and Inclusion reinforce each other.

SHD REFRAME INTAKE FORM

Desired Outcome:

Situation:

Environment:

Problem Statement:

THE SHD REFRAMING PROCESS

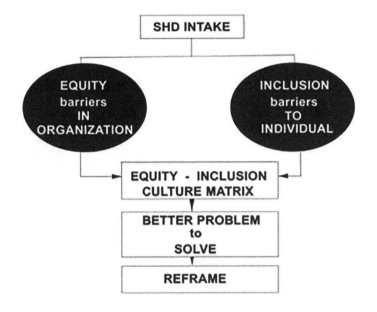

SAFE HAVEN DIALOGUES' REFRAMING PROCESS

PART TWO

THE CASES

All of the cases are based on interviews of individuals who volunteered to participate in the Safe Haven Dialogues' Reframing Process. Some wanted to learn how they could have handled a previous problem and others needed help with a current problem. The JA case is an exception. It is a composite of a couple of cases that we use as a teaching case. For this reason, it is the first in the series of cases.

It will also be noted that many of these cases deal with individuals in the **Deqin-Psychologically Toxic Cultures**. This is no surprise as these are Aggrieved Individuals who often do not have easy access to ready solutions.

SYSTEMIC DISCRIMINATION: CASE STUDY # 1 – JA

DESIRED OUTCOME:

- I want to work in a professional, inclusive environment.
- I would like XYZ company to compensate me for discriminating against me.
- XYZ company should change policies and procedures to reflect zero tolerance for discrimination.

SITUATION:

- My name is JA.
- I am a Muslim, born in Morocco.
- I migrated to the US 20 years ago and began working for a small, family-owned company.
- The company sponsored me through the H-1B visa program.
- I have a 17-year-old daughter who is about to graduate high school.
- I was initially a bus driver, then advanced to maintenance technician.
- I went to night school and currently have a Bachelor's Degree in Engineering and 2 Master's Degrees, one of which is in Project Management.
- I have been called many derogatory names by co-workers, including 'towel head' and 'camel jockey'.
- I reported incidences of racial/ethnic harassment to my managers and supervisors.
- I was told that my co-workers were just joking.
- No action has been taken by my bosses.
- Last year, I applied for a vacancy within the company.

- It would have meant a promotion and higher salary for me.
- I did not get the job.
- An external candidate with less experience and training was hired.
- I was surprised I was asked to train the new person, who was to be my senior, in aspects of Project Management.
- Yesterday, I arrived at work early and was told, without explanation, to start my shift.
- Other co-workers present were not asked to do the same.
- When I refused, I was threatened that I would be written up for insubordination.

ENVIRONMENT:

- There is a lack of supervision by managers at my workplace.
- My co-workers who are mostly male behave like 'frat boys.'
- They are verbally abusive to the few minorities who work at my job and when confronted, they make the excuse that they were joking.
- My manager socializes with my other co-workers. They frequently go to the bars for Happy Hour. I do not drink so I am never invited on these trips. I do not feel like I am part of the team.

PROBLEM STATEMENT:

XYZ company has discriminated against me:

- By denying me promotion for a job for which I am qualified.
- By expecting me to train a less qualified person for the position that I was denied, and
- By allowing a hostile work environment in which my manager and co-workers constantly racially and ethnically harass me.

ISSUES SURROUNDING INCLUSION:

Microassaults:

- JA was called derisive nicknames like "camel jockey."

- Without explanation, JA's supervisor demanded he start work earlier while other co-workers were not asked to do the same.
- JA was threatened with being "written up" for insubordination when he refused to start work earlier than his shift time.

Microinsults:

- JA was habitually referred to as "towel head" and "camel jockey" by his co-workers.

Microinvalidations:

- JA was denied promotion but a less qualified person was hired for the position and he was then asked to train that person.
- JA was excluded from socializing with his co-workers after work. This lack of inclusion caused him to feel less valued than his peers.
- JA was forced to start work earlier than his co-workers and without explanation.

ISSUES SURROUNDING EQUITY:

Privilege/Preferences:

- JA was forced to start work earlier than his scheduled time while White co-workers were not asked to do the same. When he refused he was threatened with being written up for insubordination. This demonstrates inequities in the way assignments were distributed.
- The boss showed preference to some White males by inviting them to go drinking with him after work, while JA was not invited.
- The boss did not express disapproval to those employees who called JA inappropriate names. This revealed either an insensitivity on the part of the boss, or reinforced that the other employees were privileged and hence could treat JA inappropriately.
- JA compared the behavior of his co-workers to that of 'frat boys'. This speaks of privilege.

Processes:

- There was a lack of transparency in the way promotions were decided – JA was not told why he was not promoted despite being eminently qualified for the new position. It appeared that the manager believed that JA was qualified as he was asked to coach the new hire.
- There seemed to be a lack of an appeal process for JA to question why he did not get the job.
- There does not seem to be a code of conduct about appropriate ways to address each other in the workplace. The mistreatment of others seemed to be pervasive and directed at the few minority employees.

Prospects:

- In the current environment, there is a lack of transparency regarding the importance of qualifications and excellence in determining promotions.
- JA's manager encouraged and participated in after-work socialization which excluded him. Social interactions serve to cement relationships among those who participate and exclude those who do not. JA appeared to fall under the latter category.
- JA's manager tacitly encouraged name-calling by other employees - no report was made to prove that he made any attempt to reprimand the verbal abuse.
- Given the above, JA was unable to thrive under the current circumstances.

EQUITY-INCLUSION CULTURE MATRIX

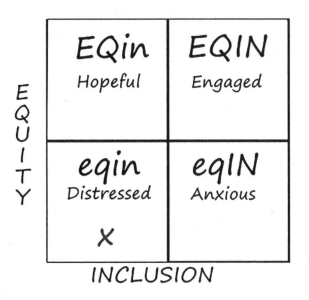

A review of the Equity-Inclusion Culture Matrix reveals that JA scores low on both the Equity and Inclusion parameters (**eqin**). He has been overlooked in favor of an external hire with lower qualifications. The organization's **Processes** are opaque and his **Prospects** for advancement are poor. He is excluded from after-work socialization, endures **Microassaults** and **Microinsults** in the form of demeaning name-calling, and is expected to train a new hire for a position for which he has been rejected.

Microinsults and **Microinvalidations** are strong. Thus, JA is working in a **Deqin-Psychologically Toxic Culture**. His Loss of Voice is complete. He is afraid to represent himself. No allies, who could speak on his behalf, are apparent. Loss of Voice at the third level exists, as no processes, such as Human Resources, that could help him, seemed to be readily available or accessible.

Since JA now has two Masters of Science degrees, his ability to find another job in a different company should be much greater. However,

JA feels somewhat trapped. His 17-year-old daughter will soon be going to college, and he needs both his present income and the benefits that he has accrued over the 20 years that he has worked for the company. He does not have 'A Hopeful Plan to Endure the Pain.' In addition, the company had sponsored his H-1B visa, which permitted him to work and live in the US.

A BETTER PROBLEM TO SOLVE:

XYZ Company is a small, family-owned entity and many of the individuals have worked for the company for several years. Minorities seem to be subjected to disrespect and ridicule.

There are two major problems. One is that the company's Rules and Regulations with respect to hiring and promotion are not transparent. The second is that there does not appear to be a Code of Conduct policy, or it is not enforced.

It appears that the owner of this small company had not set the tone and focus for Equity in the company. This suggests that JA's Desired Outcome to have rules and regulations that allow no discrimination is probably unlikely to be achieved in a realistic timeframe. Similarly, receiving compensation is unlikely in the short term as it might require involvement of an attorney.

JA's desire to work in a professional environment presents an opportunity to focus on Inclusion. There are other minorities in the organization who would benefit from an improvement in Inclusion.

A major opportunity lies in the fact that the manager had asked JA to help the new hire with Project Management tasks. JA could offer to give sessions in Project Management to members of the department on a voluntary basis. A Dialogue with the manager around increasing motivation and engagement of the employees and the potential benefit to the company is a realistic, although perhaps difficult, approach. JA should explain to the manager how his training and his Masters of Science degrees can facilitate these skill-building sessions. The possibility for benefit to individual members and to the unit could be persuasive and realistic.

If the manager accepts JA's suggestion, with respect to the training sessions in Project Management, this could potentially lead to a new job and increase of compensation for JA. The success of this Dialogue with his manager would move JA to an **AeqIN-Psychologically Unsafe Culture**, which is far better than the **Deqin-Psychologically Toxic Culture**, in which he currently resides.

THE REFRAMED PROBLEM:

JA should take a copy of Gallup's 2022 report to the meeting with his manager. He should tell his manager that he thinks that he and his co-workers could increase their productivity as is described in the Gallup report. One way to get increased engagement is to make everyone feel a part of the group and that all ideas are welcome. He should suggest that the manager appoint someone to help the group with the behaviors needed to improve engagement and motivation. He should also ask the manager to hold a special luncheon where all members of the unit could re-introduce themselves to the group in an effort to get to know more about each other's backgrounds and cultures.

JA should also explain to his boss, that although the other employees consider the name calling a joke, he and other minorities find it degrading and insulting. Finally, he should point out that in the interest of collegiality and a cooperative work environment, the manager could ask everyone to be respectful of each other.

The Reframed Problem is to persuade the manager to improve the motivation and productivity of the work unit.

This might not be an easy discussion to have with the manager, but it can be done in a non-threatening manner. JA might need some coaching to prepare him for this dialogue with his manager.

SYSTEMIC DISCRIMINATION: CASE STUDY # 2 – KD

DESIRED OUTCOME:

- To be treated fairly and to have a Human Resources department that is helpful to the workers.

SITUATION:

- I am an RN with 2 years of clinical experience.
- I am employed at a Skilled and Long-Term Wound Care facility where the Nursing Director and many Nursing colleagues are African American.
- My team consists of 1 White registered nurse (RN), 1 White certified nursing assistant (CNA), 1 Black licensed practical nurse (LPN) and I, a Black RN.
- 3 weeks after I was hired, a White RN with a Master's degree and no prior clinical experience in wound healing was hired as Unit Manager.
- The new Manager was unable/unsure how to assess patients and treat wounds so I took the lead.
- Upon completion of the assessment and treatment of a patient, the manager questioned why a clinical note documenting the treatment I had administered was necessary.
- In the ensuing weeks, she continued to demonstrate a lack of knowledge and began to become defensive and even angry that her deficits were obvious to all.
- She became increasingly hostile towards me after the addition of 2 more White RNs.

- I received more difficult assignments. She scrutinized my documentation closely and she frequently drew red lines under my wound measurements.
- She also retaliated by refusing my requests for time off.
- On one occasion, Human Resources (HR) had to intervene so that I could keep an appointment to retrieve replacement tags for my car.
- She documented unauthorized absences against me if she did not see my car in the parking lot even though colleagues attested to my being at work the entire shift.
- After HR's intervention, she called me at home expressing displeasure that I had involved that department in our dispute.
- The harassment continued with her delaying providing my work schedule in a timely fashion.
- I requested 2 days off from work, one month in advance of the designated time, and informed my manager that I was working at another hospital, and had committed to those days.
- Upon my return to work, I was summoned into the Nursing Director's office and was told I was being suspended.
- I did not receive a written warning as is customary.
- I was advised to remove my belongings from my locker.
- My manager followed me into the locker room berating me and intimating that I had made a mistake in challenging her authority.
- I succumbed to ensuing rage and pushed her forcibly out of my way and was then accosted by a Security Guard.
- I was charged with assault and lost the case and my job.
- Fortunately, the Judge refused to have my nursing license rescinded as my manager requested.

ENVIRONMENT:

- Columbia is a 300-bed hospital bed in the downtown area of a large city.
- It is known for its Wound Care and Skilled and Long-Term Care facility.

- The patient population consisted mostly of trauma victims, many of whom suffered from gunshot wounds.
- The patient demographic was working-class poor.
- The nursing staff consisted of 50% Whites and 50% Blacks.
- The Black Nursing Director and HR appeared to side with White managers most of the time.
- HR was slow to respond to employee complaints and showed little empathy.
- There were no opportunities to escalate complaints beyond HR, except to EEOC.
- The White staff appeared not to suffer from retribution from the manager.

PROBLEM STATEMENT:

- There is a failure of administration and HR to admit wrongdoing and stop the harassment of employees.

ISSUES SURROUNDING INCLUSION:

Microassaults:

- The White manager expressed annoyance on being reminded of the need to document the assessment and treatment of patients' wounds.
- The manager retaliated by assigning KD more difficult patients.
- She also did not provide KD with her weekly work schedule in a timely fashion.
- In addition, she denied KD's requests for time off.
- She refused KD's request for time off to work at another hospital, although the request was made one month in advance.
- She was unnecessarily confrontational and warned KD that she would lose any battles with her.
- She continued to needle KD as she was emptying her locker to leave the hospital after her suspension.

Microinsults:

- No **microinsults** were reported.

Microinvalidations:

- The Nursing Director summarily suspended KD without warning.
- KD's work schedules were delayed.
- KD was inhibited from scheduling work at another hospital because her primary work schedule was delayed.

ISSUES SURROUNDING EQUITY:

Privilege/Preferences:

- Although the Nursing Director was Black, she showed a preference for White RNs.
- Human Resources appeared to cater to White managers.

Processes:

- The Nursing Director and the HR department seemed to be partial to White leaders.
- White manager increased her hostility to KD after KD complained to HR.
- HR seemed slow to react to issues and showed little empathy.
- There appeared to be no internal opportunity to escalate issues above HR.

Prospects:

- Given that the control of reward and punishment was solely in the hands of the White manager, there seemed to be no positive prospects for KD.

EQUITY – INCLUSION CULTURE MATRIX

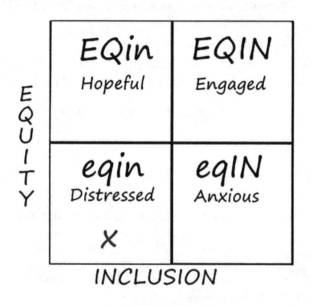

KD was in a **Deqin - Psychologically Toxic Culture. Microassaults** were strong and numerous. Given the personal nature of the conflict between KD and her White manager, there could be no resolution without intervention from the hospital administration. HR did not become involved in this conflict and KD had no Opportunity to raise it with another mediator, for example, an Ombudsman. This suggests that Processes were very poor in this Hospital. This Situation, together with the poor Prospects for KD, demonstrates that Equity was very low. Loss of Voice was complete for KD.

KD described that she could 'feel the anger rise' within her. This suggests that she could not represent her situation dispassionately enough to be heard. There seemed to be no ally who had come forward to help her, although others had complained about the clinical deficiencies of the manager. As mentioned, there was no clear process that could give voice to her problem. Further, KD had no clear 'Hopeful Plan to Endure the Pain' of her daily reality.

A BETTER PROBLEM TO SOLVE:

KD's Desired Outcome of getting an HR department that was helpful opened the possibility that this would have benefitted many employees. A major overhaul of HR, however, was unlikely to occur within a realistic timeframe and would require significant intervention. Several complaints about the White manager's lack of clinical expertise were made to the Director of Nursing, and apparently, to no avail.

Addressing the management skills of the White manager was one potential problem to solve. The fact that the Director of Nursing was Black might have explained why there was no action to improve the clinical or management skills of the White manager.

Another potential problem to solve was a mediated dialogue between KD and her manager. Given the intensity of personal animosity between both individuals, this would have required a professional intervention.

Nonetheless, KD had some potential allies. These included the other members of the team who had complained about the manager's clinical deficits and the Nursing Director, who was Black. Both could have reinforced KD's voice. KD's team members could have worked with her to present a case to the Nursing Director whose responsibility was to resolve such problems. This problem could have been addressed and would have benefited both the wound-healing team and the patients in their care.

Finally, faced with an unexpected suspension without the customary warning, the Better Problem to Solve for KD was to obtain professional guidance, internally, or ultimately from EEOC, on ways to address the situation.

THE REFRAMED PROBLEM:

KD's Reframed Problem requires an intervention. She should request Senior Management address the issues of Equity in the department. KD should seek expert guidance on how to engage senior management in this issue of Equity and how to appeal the suspension decision internally. If this is not feasible, she should pursue resolution through external agencies. This is necessary because the environment will still be unchanged on her return after her suspension if there is no intervention. An opportunity to appeal the decision would have the following benefits:

1) It would have helped to channel KD's anger.
2) It would have shone a light on the conflict between KD and her manager and thus exposed the managerial and clinical deficiencies of the supervisor. This also could have led to an assessment of the impact this conflict was having on the engagement of other members of the wound-healing department, and more importantly, on patient care.

Unfortunately, this option was not pursued, and the outcome was quite negative for KD.

SYSTEMIC DISCRIMINATION: CASE STUDY # 3 – TB

DESIRED OUTCOME:

- To be accepted and respected for my abilities and achievements.

SITUATION:

- My name is TB and I am employed by a small (about 200 employees), domestic organization as a Human Resources (HR) specialist.
- I have an MBA in Human Resources Management and 8-10 years of prior experience as a Resource Manager.
- On my second day of employment, my supervisor asked, "Would you like to be addressed by another name?"
- My name is not a common American name.
- I responded: "I would like to be called by my given name – the name by which I am known."
- After changing my hairstyle to a more natural look, my supervisor asked whether my hair was a weave.
- She then proceeded to tell me my hair was too big for her liking.
- The following day she invited me to lunch.
- Under the guise of offering advice, she remarked that I needed to work on my very southern accent and indicated it was difficult to understand because "southerners tend to use figurative language."
- She added that other Blacks had adapted their language and style to fit into the culture of the organization.
- I was very sensitive to the accent issue because, ever since I heard myself over a loudspeaker, I felt I did not have the

best-sounding speaking voice. People often say: "you have a distinctive voice," which I often took as a negative comment.

- I called a friend and shared with her some of the comments from my supervisor. Her response was – "Girl, you need to get out of there."
- In my capacity as an HR specialist, an employee came to me and complained that her supervisor had created a hostile environment, which made it difficult for her to work constructively.
- I investigated the situation, documented comments from the witnesses, wrote up my findings, and gave them to the supervisor's manager, as was the HR practice.
- The supervisor's manager complained that I was too aggressive in reporting the incident and I was hostile to the supervisor.
- I pointed out that it was the employee who had complained that her boss had created a hostile environment.
- My supervisor reprimanded me and told me that I should have asked permission to submit the 'write-up' since it concerned a White male.
- I was informed that I needed to attend a course on Employee Relations.
- My supervisor also took away some of my responsibilities.
- I became very depressed and sought professional help and informed my supervisor I was in therapy.
- A few days later, I was stunned when a White male employee told me that he had learned that I had a mental problem.
- I advised my supervisor that it was not only inappropriate for her to have shared my health issue, but also illegal.
- I complained to the CEO who told me that the White employee only said it out of concern for me.
- The CEO refused to deal with this breach of confidentiality.
- I also received informal feedback that I was arrogant, too direct, too aggressive, and came off as being angry.
- I began to feel like I had a target on my back.
- On the one hand, my supervisor was bringing minor errors to my attention.

- At the same time, I was being assigned the most complex cases, because 'I had the most experience' among the small HR team.
- About this time, one of my colleagues left because of similar treatment, and a colleague of Arabic ethnicity was hired. I was tasked with training her.
- Shortly thereafter, the CEO held a Zoom meeting for all employees to discuss the George Floyd murder.
- A few Blacks and Hispanics made comments. An older Black mother began crying and explained that every time her son is out, she fears he might come to a similar fate as George Floyd.
- The CEO responded, "Everyone of color – you need to get yourself together and get back to work."
- I was so distraught that I became tearful. Immediately afterward, I took a 3-month leave of absence.
- On my return, my supervisor indicated that I had a number of 'performance issues' and they had decided to give me a separation package.
- I accepted the package but wished I had stood my ground.
- As a strong Black woman once said, "If you want to be the last one standing, stand in your truth!"

ENVIRONMENT:

- The organization employs about 200 people, 17% of whom are Black.
- All top executives are White except for the Executive Director of HR. who is Black.
- She was what was described as an 'acceptable Negro.' Of the remaining Black HR Managers, two were 'acceptable Negroes', and the colleague who left and I were the other two Blacks in the HR department.
- There were no White employees in the HR department.
- HR Department did not make decisions based on HR practices. It basically rubber-stamped the wishes of the leaders of the departments.

- Black and Hispanic employees were constantly under pressure not to make mistakes while White employees received many chances.
- For example, a White male, who was caught embezzling funds from the company, was not fired. He was 'downsized' and allowed to collect unemployment.

PROBLEM STATEMENT:

- The company did not allow true Diversity and opportunities for minorities.

ISSUES SURROUNDING INCLUSION:

Microassaults:

- TB's supervisor implied that she should change her name to one that was more commonly known.
- TB was told to adapt her style and language to fit the White culture of the company.
- Her supervisor commented on her natural hairstyle and advised her to work on her southern accent.
- A White male employee told her that he had heard that she had a mental problem.
- TB was forced to take a course in Employee Relations.
- She was stereotyped as the 'angry Black Woman.'
- She was punished for using standard Human Resources methods to investigate a complaint against a White male supervisor.

Microinsults:

- Within the first few days of her employment, TB was confronted with disturbing examples of **microaggressions**, including comments on wearing her hair natural, being asked to call herself by a different name, and being told to change her Southern accent.
- She was told to adapt her style and language to fit the White culture.

- TB had to endure her CEO saying People of Color needed to get themselves together and get back to work.
- TB was perceived as arrogant and angry and felt the sting of the 'angry Black woman' stereotype.

Microinvalidations:

- TB was forced to be other than her authentic self.
- She was punished for using standard HR methods to investigate a complaint.
- Her responsibilities were reduced.
- She was reprimanded for not asking permission to investigate and deliver a report on a White supervisor.
- She was told to take a course in Employee Relations as punishment for submitting a report on a White male supervisor.

ISSUES SURROUNDING EQUITY:

Privilege/Preferences:

- TB was punished for investigating a complaint against a White male manager.
- White employee who had committed fraud was treated leniently and allowed to leave the organization without a stain on his record.
- Black employees were treated more harshly when they transgressed.
- CEO held a meeting to talk about George Floyd and when an elderly employee expressed her fear that her son might suffer a similar fate, the CEO advised all employees of color to "pull themselves together and get back to work."
- Except for the Director of HR, managers were White.

Processes:

- HR department was subservient to the White managers.
- Standard HR methods were not practiced.
- On her return from a leave of absence, her supervisor gave her a separation package because she had 'performance issues'.

Prospects:

- TB was not only reprimanded for her 'write up' of a White manager against whom a complaint was made, but her responsibilities were also reduced.

EQUITY – INCLUSION CULTURE MATRIX:

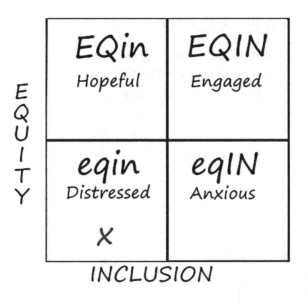

Equity was very low, and the presence of Privilege and poor Processes led to poor Prospects for TB. In this organization, the role of the HR department was, unfortunately, to serve the desires of the White managers. White managers were treated as a privileged group. HR Processes were not observed. Blacks were only tolerated if they were assimilating and adapting to the predominant White culture. In fact, TB's expertise and experience as an HR specialist seemed comparatively less important. This was an incredibly strong **microinvalidation** of TB's achievements. The **microaggressions** against TB were pervasive.

The lack of empathy displayed by the CEO, in response to the elderly Black employee, epitomized the toxicity of the culture. This behavior reflected a culture of low Inclusion and low Equity. TB suffered Loss of Voice at the first level, as no one was sympathetic to her concerns. She had no allies and her ability to assimilate was extremely important to her Black supervisor. Loss of Voice at the third level existed as there were no processes designed to give her complaints an independent and fair hearing. TB also had no 'Hopeful Plan to Endure the Pain.' As a result, she suffered significant emotional distress. TB is a Distressed Individual in a **Deqin- Psychologically Toxic Culture**.

A BETTER PROBLEM TO SOLVE:

TB's Desired Outcome was to be accepted and respected for her abilities. The presence of strong **microinvalidations** in which her expertise was not only rejected, but also resented, suggest that this was not a realistic Desired Outcome. As a result, it could not have been achieved in a realistic time frame. It was also unlikely that TB could have had a realistic Dialogue about her Desired Outcome because for her manager, becoming an 'acceptable Black' was the basis for success. There is no sense that the CEO or White managers were interested in creating Engaged Employees. TB had become physically ill and emotionally distressed in this Psychologically Toxic Culture.

TB should have used her 3-month 'Leave of Absence' to find employment at a less toxic company! Before leaving. she could have challenged both the Head of HR and the CEO about the sharing of her health information.

THE REFRAMED PROBLEM:

- Find a job at a company with a Psychologically Safe Culture, ASAP.

SYSTEMIC DISCRIMINATION: CASE STUDY # 4 – BR

DESIRED OUTCOME:

- To be treated fairly and retained in the Office Manager position.

SITUATION:

- My name is BR and I am employed in Enrollment Services of a Community College for the past 3 years.
- I applied for an Office Manager position responsible for Enrollment at one of the satellite sites of the College. This would have been a promotion that could have resulted in an increase in pay and grade.
- I was transferred to the satellite office as Assistant Manager.
- Three weeks later, a White coworker was transferred as Manager and became the boss for the Enrollment Office of this Satellite site.
- I was not given a logical or truthful explanation about why I was not given the position.
- I have an Associate's Degree and have been working towards my Bachelor's Degree.
- I have over 15 years of customer service experience and, as a military wife, served in military sites in many states and Europe. This Satellite site was close to a military site.
- My new boss has a secretarial certification, but no degree.
- She has worked in different areas of the main campus over a 10-year period. Because she was not familiar with Enrollment Services, I ended up running the office including making the critical decisions.

- My boss was frequently absent from the office and spent a lot of her time fraternizing with the soldiers and young professors. She acted as though the job was 'beneath her.'
- I complained to her Boss, who was not only unsympathetic but 'wrote me up' for insubordination.
- Included in the letter was a complaint from a student that I was tardy in resolving his issue. It was placed in my file and Human Resources (HR) stated that there was little that they could do.
- I discovered an opening in a different department on the main campus. It was in Accounting Services and although a lateral move by grade and title, it actually paid more because it dealt with budgets.
- I remained in this department before relocating to another state to work as an Addiction Counselor, having attained my Master's Degree, in the interim.

ENVIRONMENT:

- There are about 5000 students in three satellite sites.
- At the time of this incident, there were about 300 employees, 15 of whom were Hispanics and 7 were Black.
- Most leaders were White.
- HR focused on hiring, firing and promotion processes. They were all White.
- There was one person in HR who was well known to be fair and tried to help employees.
- The rest 'did not give a damn'.
- If an employee was considered a top performer, transferring to other departments was possible, but climbing the ladder was difficult.
- On occasion, managers would take employees' ideas and not give them credit for it.

PROBLEM STATEMENT:

- There is a lack of clarity and transparency in evaluation processes and handling of complaints.

ISSUES SURROUNDING INCLUSION:

Microassaults:

- Being written up for insubordination.
- A White co-worker with less qualifications and experience was hired for the job for which BR had applied.
- HR placed a questionable complaint from a student in BR's file.
- BR's boss frequently socialized while BR performed the work her boss was incapable of doing.

Microinsults:

- No reports of **microinsults.**

Microinvalidations:

- Managers at BR's workplace took credit for contributions from others.
- A White co-worker with lower academic credentials and experience was hired instead of BR.
- BR had to assume responsibility for Enrollment Services because her new boss did not have the experience or skills to perform the job for which she was hired.

ISSUES SURROUNDING EQUITY:

Privilege/Preferences:

- There was a preference for White co-workers.

Processes:

- HR focused on hiring, promotions etc. but put little effort into helping employees.
- Lateral moves were possible, but 'climbing the ladder' was impossible.
- There was no transparency and explanation for the hiring decisions made at this institution.

Prospects:

- Lateral moves were possible for good performers.
- There was no opportunity for upward mobility.

EQUITY-INCLUSION CULTURE MATRIX

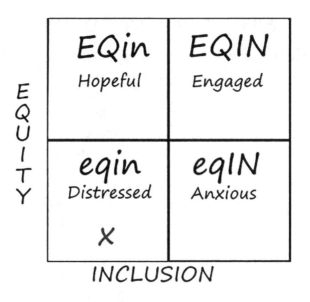

An examination of the Equity axis reveals that Equity is low. Whites are privileged and preferentially receive managerial jobs, regardless of the qualifications of the BIPOC candidates. As a result, Prospects for BR are capped at Assistant Manager positions, apparently throughout the entire system. This is further worsened by the fact that there are no HR systems to deal with personnel issues outside of hiring, promotions, and firing.

On the Inclusion axis, the situation of BR having to work on Enrollment issues that her boss was hired to do, makes the **microaggressions** difficult for BR to endure. BR has a Loss of Voice in that the HR system did not deal with personnel discrimination issues, and there was no other system to support employees with similar problems.

Although BR did not articulate a clear 'Hopeful Plan to Endure the Pain', she was working on a Master's degree. The potential to make lateral movements to other departments opened the possibility of finding Cultures with more favorable Inclusion practices. BR is a Distressed individual in a **Deqin-Psychologically Toxic Culture**.

A BETTER PROBLEM TO SOLVE:

BR's Desired Outcome to achieve a managerial position seems unrealistic in a short time-frame. It is also not a dialogue that she can have with her present boss, given both the low Equity for BIPOC individuals in the overall organization and the relationship between her and her boss. Processes did enable lateral moves and strong performers were validated by being allowed to make such transfers.

This intersection of Equity and Inclusion offers the possibility that BR could move to the **AeqIN** quadrant if she is able to transfer to a department where the manager encourages Behaviors of Inclusion. Thus, a Better Problem to Solve is transferring to another department where her expertise and contributions would be valued. This would increase the Inclusion component because of the validation and acceptance of her contributions. This is more predictable than depending on a particular individual to make specific changes to increase Equity in the organization. Of interest, BR had a Hopeful Plan to Endure the Pain. She was working on her Master's Degree with the intent of changing careers.

THE REFRAMED PROBLEM:

As described above, BR should seek to transfer to a department where her expertise is recognized and valued. This was what she did successfully.

SYSTEMIC DISCRIMINATION: CASE STUDY # 5 – DR. JD

DESIRED OUTCOME:

- Discipline the offender by placing him on probation and/or firing him.
- Review/retrain the staff regarding policies and procedures related to discharging patients from the Emergency Department.

SITUATION:

- I am Dr. JD, a Black attending physician and I work in the Emergency Department of a large hospital.
- I evaluated a high-risk Hispanic patient with chest pain and determined the patient should be admitted to the hospital.
- I informed Dr. H., a third-year resident on the Medicine Service, that the patient had been admitted to the hospital and he should do the onboarding interview.
- Dr. H. came down to the Emergency Department (ED), saw the patient and discharged the patient from the hospital.
- Once I noticed that the patient was getting dressed, I attempted to approach the patient at bedside.
- I was physically blocked by Dr. H. who prevented me from talking to my patient.
- Additionally, Dr. H. grabbed my arm in an aggressive manner to prevent me from moving forward.
- I wrote an incident report and submitted it to the hospital administrator and sent a copy to my boss.
- The next day, the chairman of my department met with me to discuss the incident.

- He suggested that I attend a meeting with Dr. H. and the hospital psychiatrist. I declined.
- Later that day, as news of the interaction spread, one White female colleague suggested that there was not much that could be done about the interaction.
- A second female colleague opined that I should have flopped on the floor and created a ruckus but barring that not much could be done.
- Over the ensuing 2-3 weeks, my boss arranged a meeting with Dr. H. and the head of his department.
- At the meeting, Dr. H.'s Department Head told me that he had spoken to several members of the hospital staff both in the ED and on the Medicine service who advised that I was a good person and had no difficulty with any staff members.
- He also indicated that Dr. H. was a star resident who was doing important research at the hospital.
- At the meeting Dr. H. passed me a letter in which he "apologized" for upsetting me but indicated that I had misconstrued the situation.
- The meeting lasted 30 minutes, after which I left the room.

ENVIRONMENT:

- Helping Hands Hospital is a busy inner-city hospital whose patient population is mostly poor/ blue-collar, working-class minorities.
- The hospital is staffed by residents with attending physicians who are a phone call away except in the ED, where attending physicians supervise residents onsite 24 hours/day.
- Attending Physicians determine which patients get admitted to the hospital from the ED.
- I am the only Black attending physician in the department.
- There were 2 previous Black attending physicians, one of whom was female and had experienced intense discrimination and the other was a Black male physician who had been mentored by the head of the department and had been very popular with colleagues and staff.

- Within the Emergency Department, Research is considered important but is not necessary.

PROBLEM STATEMENT:

- My position as attending physician has been undermined by a resident and the heads of departments at this hospital.
- A subordinate has ignored my instructions and then attempted to physically restrain me. He has suffered no real consequences.

ISSUES SURROUNDING INCLUSION:

Microassaults:

- Dr. H. grabbed Dr. JD's arm in an aggressive manner. Technically, this was an assault.
- The suggestion by the chairman that Dr. JD meet with a psychiatrist was an assault on her professionalism and her psyche.
- Dr. H.'s apology letter in which he claimed that Dr. JD had misconstrued his intent added 'insult to injury.'

Microinsults:

- Dr. H. not only refused to carry out Dr. JD's order, but also defied it and made his own decision. He did this either because she was female or Black.
- The chairman of Dr. JD's department does not treat her with respect as a professional. Another Black female attending physician experienced significant discrimination.
- The chairman further insulted Dr. JD by suggesting that she and Dr. H. should have a meeting with the psychiatrist.
- The suggestion of a visit to the psychiatrist reinforced the stereotype of the 'angry Black woman.'

Microinvalidations:

- The chairman of Dr. JD's department does not treat her with the respect that she has earned as an attending physician.

- Dr. H.'s actions indicated a refusal to acknowledge and accept Dr. JD's seniority and authority.
- He treated Dr. JD as though she were the junior physician and refused to recognize her authority and responsibility to admit and discharge patients from the Emergency Department.
- Dr. H.'s decision to reverse Dr. JD's order to admit the patient, and then to make a unilateral decision to discharge the patient, was an affront to Dr. JD's standing and authority.

ISSUES SURROUNDING EQUITY:

Privilege/Preferences:

- Dr. H. was known for questioning decisions made by other physicians.
- The physician who said that Dr. JD should have raised 'holy hell' was a White female who knew that it would not have been tolerated, had Dr. H. assaulted a White female physician.
- Dr. H. was allowed to behave inappropriately because the hospital valued his research activity.
- Researchers seemed to be valued more than clinicians.
- Dr. H showed little concern for this Hispanic patient.
- The excellent reputation that Dr. JD had, with respect to interactions with other staff, did not provide her benefit of the doubt.

Processes:

- There seems to be no process for enforcing hospital rules governing decision-making, with respect to patients.
- Resolution of conflicts appears to be situation-based as opposed to being guided by established rules.
- Resolution of conflicts appears to depend on the status level of individuals.
- There does not seem to be a review process for decisions made on patients with potentially serious conditions.
- There are no guidelines governing attending/resident or insubordinate interactions.

- The Human Resources department seemed not to play a role.
- Individuals do not seem to have a safe place to discuss difficult personnel issues.

Prospects:

- The prospects for Dr. H. seem to be excellent as he was valued for his research activity and supported by the chairman of his department.
- The prospects for Dr. JD seem to be compromised as she is not supported by her own chairman, and he has diminished her by not reinforcing her authority as an Attending Physician.
- The action of Dr. JD's chairman also reduced the respect that hospital staff in the ED had for her.
- Dr. JD's reputation and authority as an Attending Physician in the ED has been undermined by a lack of rebuke for Dr. H.'s behavior.

EQUITY – INCLUSION CULTURE MATRIX:

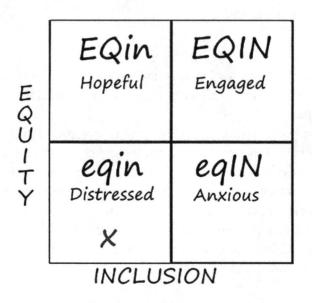

Equity in this organization is compromised by several circumstances. These include the absence of, or lack of adherence to, protocols and rules that specify chain of command, authority, and responsibility in the ED. The existence of Privilege, such as that which was bestowed on the resident, Dr. H., due to his research activity, was another feature of low Equity. The latter improved his Prospects, while by implication, the lack of research activity on Dr. JD's part did not improve her Prospects. The **microinsults** and **microinvalidation** experienced by Dr. JD spoke to her not being treated with the respect normally associated with her professional status.

At the point of this event, Dr. JD is in a **Deqin-Psychologically Toxic Culture**. This was not associated with a Loss of Voice in that Dr. JD could represent her problem and evoke a reaction to find a solution from the Chairmen of the two departments involved. The fact that Dr. H. offered a half-hearted apology, does not detract from a positive response on the Equity axis, even though the Privilege given to Dr. H. dampens the effectiveness of the apology. Nonetheless, this moves

Dr. JD into an **AeqIN-Psychologically Unsafe Culture**. Much of her anxiety comes from the unpredictability of the Equity policies and the resulting **microaggressions** from subordinates, such as Dr. H.

It should also be mentioned that although Dr. JD had a 'Hopeful Plan to Endure the Pain' by ultimately moving to a different hospital, the successful achievement of this Plan depended on Letters of References from at least one of these department chairmen.

Interestingly, the care and disposition of the patient, who was at the center of this event, was neither emphasized by Dr. JD nor the Chairmen of the two departments. This underscores the collateral damage that frequently occurs but is often unrecognized or ignored in **Deqin-Psychologically Toxic Cultures**.

A BETTER PROBLEM TO SOLVE:

Dr. JD has two Desired Outcomes. One outcome is the significant disciplining of Dr. H and the other is reviewing and reinforcing the procedures that govern discharging patients from the ER. Common issues around Inclusion and Equity, in this case, are the processes and behaviors that accrue to the benefit of the Privileged. These issues affected the professional and health aspects of a Black female physician and a Hispanic patient, respectively. These two issues could result, not only in damage to patients who are treated inappropriately in the ED, but also in significant legal costs to the hospital. The potential impact on the health of patients and legal action against the hospital provide the opportunity for improving productivity in the Emergency Department.

The Better Problem to Solve is the reviewing and strengthening of the rules governing discharge of patients from the ED; identifying the chain of command; and resolving decision-making conflicts over discharge of patients from the ED. First, this will benefit countless patients who visit the ED with illnesses that involve varying medical disciplines. Second, it will make clear the chain of command, the system for conflict resolution, and the penalties for transgressing this policy.

Dr. Frank L. Douglas

<u>THE REFRAMED PROBLEM:</u>

The Reframed Problem is the rapid implementation of rules governing discharge of patients from the ED. Addressing this problem will engage all the ED Attending Physicians as well as the Chairpersons of the major medical and surgical departments. Dr. JD should volunteer to put a multidisciplinary group together to review present policies and present recommendations to the Chairpersons of the Departments for approval. Included in these recommendations, should be focus on improving the treatment of women and minority staff and patients in the ED.

There should also be training sessions to reinforce the guidelines.

SYSTEMIC DISCRIMINATION: CASE STUDY # 6 – DR. M.S.

DESIRED OUTCOME:

- Regular re-education/reorientation of the entire hospital staff on how to treat patients of different ethnicities.
- Education of physicians on **microaggressions** and methods to avoid them.
- Education of hospital staff on the impact unconscious biases have on patient care.
- Termination of the Head of Department in the Cancer Screening Center.

SITUATION:

- My name is Dr. M.S. and I am a 37-year-old married Black female physician.
- My mother has breast cancer. My aunt and cousin have both died from breast cancer.
- At 26 weeks of pregnancy, I began to bleed from my left breast.
- At the same time, I discovered a large mass in my left breast.
- My regular obstetrician was away, so the covering doctor ordered an ultrasound.
- The ultrasound technician was a Black woman who was immediately concerned by the images.
- She called the Head of Breast Cancer Screening, an Asian female physician.
- The physician looked at me, discounted the ultrasound images, and said changes appeared to be associated with pregnancy and that I should go home, massage my breast, and apply warm water compresses.

- Two weeks later, I saw my OB/GYN whom I exhorted to re-examine me despite the "negative" ultrasound.
- He immediately arranged for a breast biopsy.
- After the biopsy, a White male physician entered my room and said "You have breast cancer. I don't see how anyone could have missed this. I will take this case to Morbidity & Mortality conference.
- I listened and did not respond. He then said "Do you understand what I am saying? You need to get your husband here."
- In the aftermath, I asked about harvesting my eggs.
- "You are lucky enough to have one baby. Why would you want anymore?" – a White female oncologist asked.
- At 6.5-7 months of my pregnancy, I underwent a mastectomy.
- I enquired about whether I could breastfeed my baby. My surgeon's response – "Breast feeding is overrated."
- Post mastectomy, despite many requests, I did not receive adequate pain medication.
- I asked to be placed near the bathroom and since my surgery was on my upper body, I could easily walk unaided to the bathroom. My request was denied.
- I was subsequently discharged. Six weeks later, I was back in the same hospital to deliver my baby.
- Post-delivery, I was made to walk to my new room while my husband transported my baby in a bassinet.
- My White roommate was transported in a wheelchair with her baby.
- I was placed in a room close to the nurse's station and I could overhear the nursing staff remarking that "she says she is a doctor but I am not sure."
- At the allotted time, my roommate's baby was brought to her for feeding and when I asked where my baby was, I was told that she had already been fed.
- My baby had a heart murmur and required an ultrasound prior to discharge. I asked to go into the room while the ultrasound was being done and was immediately told I could not accompany my baby for the ultrasound.

- Finally, the charge nurse came into my room and angrily said, "When are you leaving?" "Who is the father and who is coming to sign the birth certificate?" She had mistaken me for the one other Black patient on the ward. I left the hospital that day.
- One month later, I was back for a breast cancer follow-up screening of my right breast.
- I encountered the same Black female technician who suggested I might qualify for a clinical trial that was ongoing at the institution.
- She assured me that she would call her supervisor to discuss the clinical trial with me.
- In walked the head of Department who had originally misdiagnosed my breast mass several months earlier.
- She took one look at me and said, "Clinical Trials do not take Medicaid patients."

ENVIRONMENT:

- A 1500-bed private hospital in the heart of a large urban cosmopolitan city.
- An academic-teaching institution.
- Attending physicians, residents and medical students staff the institution.
- Staff are all races and ethnicities.
- Heads of Departments are majority White males in their 60s-70s.
- Board-certified radiologists are on site during the day and read all films.
- 90% of patients have private physicians.
- Private physicians primarily care for their patients. Unfortunately, my private physician was away, so I was under the care of the hospital staff physicians.
- Except for a few specialties, attending physicians do not remain in-house 24 hours/day.
- 6% of resident physicians are Black, 18% are Asian, 2% are Hispanic, and 74% are White.
- 3% of attending physicians are Black.

- 80% of patients are White.
- Janitorial staff is mostly minority (80%).

PROBLEM STATEMENT:

- I have been discriminated against and treated differently from White patients. This inequitable treatment has resulted in substandard care and could have caused me grave injury.

ISSUES SURROUNDING INCLUSION:

Microassaults:

- Dr. M.S., a newly delivered mother, was made to walk from the delivery room to a hospital bed, while others were transported in wheelchairs.
- The nursing staff expressed skepticism that Dr. M.S. was indeed a physician.
- While other new mothers were feeding their babies, her baby was fed by someone else, thus depriving Dr. M.S. of the opportunity to bond with her newborn.
- The charge nurse openly questioned who was the baby's father and who would sign the birth certificate.
- The nursing staff did not allow the new mother to accompany her baby for ultrasound.
- The charge nurse demanded to know when Dr. M.S. was leaving the hospital.
- The head of Breast Cancer Screening misdiagnosed Dr. M.S. breast cancer, which the surgeon claimed was hard to miss. This suggested that the head of Breast Cancer Screening was not careful or lacked the knowledge to make a diagnosis and thus endangered Dr. M.S.' health.
- The assumption was made, based on the fact Dr. M.S. was Black, that she was a Medicaid patient and therefore would not qualify to be part of a clinical trial.

Microinsults:

- A male physician giving Dr. M.S. the diagnosis of breast cancer requested that her husband be present as he assumed she would not understand what he had to say.
- When Dr. M.S. asked about harvesting her eggs, she was told that she had one baby so why would she need more.
- The charge nurse questioned who the baby's father was and who was going to sign the birth certificate.
- Dr. M.S. was mistaken for the only other Black patient in the unit.
- Head of Breast Cancer Screening assumed Dr. M.S. was a Medicaid patient because she was Black and asserted that Medicaid patients didn't qualify for clinical trials.

Microinvalidations:

- A male physician requested that Dr. M.S. have her husband come into the room as he assumed that she would not understand what he had to say.
- Dr. M.S. was told that breastfeeding was overrated when she asked about breastfeeding after her mastectomy.
- The nursing staff questioned whether she was indeed a physician.
- It was assumed she was a Medicaid patient because she was Black.

ISSUES SURROUNDING EQUITY:

Privilege/Preferences:

- A wheelchair was provided to transport a White patient from the delivery unit while Dr. M.S. was made to walk to her room.
- Dr. M.S. was denied the opportunity to feed her newborn infant while a new White mother was allowed to feed her baby.
- Dr. M.S. was denied the right to be present when her newborn was being evaluated.
- Medicaid patients are not allowed to participate in clinical trials.

Processes:

- There appeared to be a lack of secondary review of abnormal findings on ultrasound.
- There was a lack of process on new baby feedings.
- There appeared to be a lack of process on allowing new mothers to be present when their babies are being evaluated.

Prospects:

- Poor medical care was provided to Black patients. A physician misinterpreted ultrasound findings of breast cancer in a patient with a strong family history of breast cancer.
- The general disrespect of this patient by physicians and nursing staff increased the potential for mistakes leading to hospital-induced problems.
- This pregnant patient was in a hostile healthcare environment which caused additional significant stress, given her new diagnosis of breast cancer.
- This patient received inadequate care that could have led to worse outcomes and further impeded her recovery.

EQUITY – INCLUSION CULTURE MATRIX:

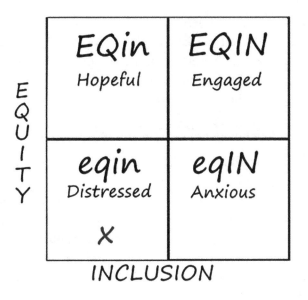

The poor treatment of Dr. M.S. compared to White patients highlights the preference that was given to White patients. There were also gaps in the processes of confirming diagnoses of significant illnesses, which exacerbated the overall lack of diligence in the care of Dr. M.S. and the potential prospect of a poor outcome. The **microaggressions** in this case read like a textbook of the **microassaults, microinsults**, and **microinvalidations** that marginalized individuals often experience in organizations where Systemic Discrimination is ignored and allowed to fester.

Dr. M.S. is in a **Deqin – Psychologically Toxic Culture** in which low Equity and low Inclusion are creating significant distress for her as a mother who is postpartum. Unfortunately, this **Deqin** Culture was not restricted to Dr. M.S. Any Black patient would probably have suffered similar discrimination. For example, Dr. M.S. was denied access to a Clinical Trial because it was assumed that she was a Medicaid patient. This is another example of healthcare disparities experienced by Black patients. The prevention of the bonding between the newborn and the mother also caused unnecessary emotional stress for Dr. M.S. and was not best practice for the care of a newborn.

The Loss of Voice in this patient is remarkable because she is a physician, who was so traumatized that she could not protect herself against the **microaggressions**, misdiagnoses, and poor medical treatment of her and her newborn. She did not have a meaningful 'Hopeful Plan to Endure the Pain' as the encounters were of finite duration.

A BETTER PROBLEM TO SOLVE:

Three of the four parts of Dr. M.S.' Desired Outcome deal with the education of the entire or sections of the staff with respect to the proper treatment of marginalized patients. Re-education should address biases based on ethnicity, gender, and economic status. Establishing a program to educate the staff about **microaggressions** and the impact of unconscious biases on patient care could be accomplished in a reasonable timeframe. Addressing this Desired Outcome would also benefit many patients, whether they be BIPOC patients or those of poor economic status. Termination of the head of the Cancer Screening Center is probably not a realistic Outcome based on the Situation described.

Since Dr. M.S. is not a member of the staff of this hospital, there is probably little that she could do to influence changes in Equity. However, she might be able to influence the improvement of Inclusion behaviors.

The question is how to have a realistic dialogue with the appropriate manager. In this case, this would be the Head of the Cancer Center or the CEO of the hospital, if needed. The organization of this dialogue is possible because Dr. M.S. is a physician. She is in a powerful position to get an audience with the leaders of the Cancer Center or the CEO. Her case is very instructive with respect to biases leading to misdiagnosis and poor postpartum and newborn care.

Hence, A Better Problem to Solve is convincing the CEO to educate the entire hospital staff on the negative impact that biases can have on the care of patients.

THE REFRAMED PROBLEM:

Dr. M.S. claimed that the differentiated treatment because of her ethnicity had caused her 'grave injury.' We would not change this problem statement. It appears Dr. M.S. was so traumatized by the mistreatment that she could not summon the 'fight' response to defend herself against the malignant attacks regarding her professional and economic status. Post-discharge, Dr. M.S. should have sought help from her colleagues and a lawyer to frame a request to the CEO of the hospital. The request should be focused on the need to implement a program to assess and reduce bias in the diagnosis and treatment of patients from marginalized groups in the Cancer Screening Center.

SYSTEMIC DISCRIMINATION: CASE STUDY # 7 – DR. GT

DESIRED OUTCOME:

- I would like to be respected as a physician.
- I would like to be treated as an equal to my peers.
- I would like there to be less hostility and more professionalism.
- I would like there to be zero tolerance for discrimination.

SITUATION:

- My name is Dr. GT and I am a fourth year Emergency Medicine resident at All Saints Hospital.
- During my four years of residency, I have been continually subjected to racial discrimination and gender bias.
- A few examples –
- Next to the attending physician, I am the most senior clinician on staff. Every day, I am faced with one or more of the following:
- I enter a patient's room with my team and introduce myself – "Good morning, I am Dr. GT. Please tell me why you are here." After a series of questions, I discuss a plan with my patient and as I am leaving the room, I hear the following: "Miss, can you tell me when the doctor is going to come in?"
  A private physician comes into the department and begins to speak to my male medical student regarding a plan of care for his patient and completely ignores me, the senior resident.
- Some of the nurses in our department continually ignore my instructions or take a long time to respond.
- During a patient encounter in the trauma bay, the trauma nurse repeatedly pushed me out of the way to attend to the patient.

- I asked her not to touch me but she continued to do so. I have not seen her do this to any other physician.
- I reported these incidents to a senior Black male physician, whom I respect.
- To my astonishment, his response implied that somehow this was my fault. He stated that the way I spoke proper English (grammatically correct and without slang) made me appear snobbish and arrogant.
- A comment made by a nurse "who does this chick think she is?" was particularly disturbing.
- The attending physician made no suggestion on how to handle the problems. His attitude was 'don't rock the boat.'
- Male surgical physicians would frequently come to the Emergency Department with their large teams and insult and degrade me in front of all my subordinates.

ENVIRONMENT:

- A large inner-city hospital.
- Most of the patients are minorities.
- 90% of the Attending Physicians are Caucasians.
- I am the second Black female resident in a newly created residency program.
- There are multiple internecine feuds between Emergency Medicine and other surgical specialties in the hospital.

PROBLEM STATEMENT:

- I feel discriminated against because of my race and gender, and I have been unable to get any help from my immediate supervisors.
- I have feelings of dread when I have to go to work and my health has been adversely affected.

ISSUES SURROUNDING INCLUSION:

Microassaults:

- Senior Black male physician told Dr. GT that her grammatically precise language made her sound arrogant and snobbish.
- Dr. GT was physically pushed aside by a trauma nurse.
- One nurse commented: 'who does this chick think she is?' when referring to Dr. GT.
- A private attending physician ignored Dr. GT and discussed his patient with the White male medical student.

Microinsults:

- No **microinsults** were reported.

Microinvalidations:

- Dr. GT's patient addressed her as 'Miss' and asked when the doctor was coming to see her.
- A private attending physician ignored Dr. GT and began discussing his patient with a male medical student.
- Nurses ignored Dr. GT's instructions or performed them reluctantly.
- A senior male medical physician signaled that Dr. GT should not rock the boat.
- The trauma nurse treated her as though she did not belong or had no right to be there.
- The male surgeons also disrespected and demeaned Dr. GT in front of their teams.

ISSUES SURROUNDING EQUITY:

Privilege/Preferences:

- White male medical students seem to be preferred over Black female physicians.
- There is a sense that male physicians, including Black male physicians are preferred over Black female physicians in this department.

- The comment made by the senior Black male physician suggests that he is an 'acceptable Black' in this organization, and therefore had no empathy for Dr. GT.

Processes:

- There seems to be no systemic processes to deal with **microaggressions**.
- There does not seem to be a set of rules guiding organizational behaviors and relationships.

Prospects:

- The lack of support and constructive guidance from the senior Black male physician suggests that the Prospects for Dr. GT in this hospital are low.

EQUITY – INCLUSION CULTURE MATRIX:

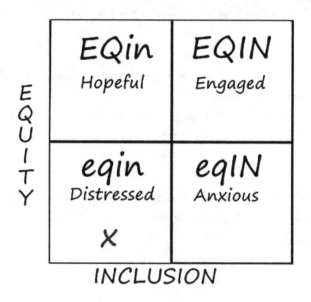

Dr. GT is in a **Deqin- Psychologically Toxic Culture**. One of the characteristics of hospitals and universities is that the departments often have their own sub-cultures, where the actual daily practices can be different from that espoused by the overall administration. In Dr. GT's situation, Inclusion behaviors were not consciously promoted and there was no structure to encourage fairness and simple mutual respect among associates.

Working in a **Deqin-Psychologically Toxic Culture** in these types of organizations can be overwhelming for the Aggrieved individual, particularly since the individual's future career can be determined by recommendations from the leaders. In this culture, there is little that Dr. GT can do directly to impact Equity.

The dependence of one's future on one or two supervisors is a major deterrent to giving voice to one's concerns. The individual power those successful supervisors might have could frustrate any endeavor on the part of the organization to maintain a good Equity-Inclusion culture.

Fortunately, possession of a 'Hopeful Plan to Endure the Pain' is helpful in these situations because time in a residency or fellowship program is finite.

A BETTER PROBLEM TO SOLVE:

Dr. GT's Desired Outcomes have a common theme of wanting to be treated professionally and with respect. She was the only Black among the 10 fourth-year Residents in the Emergency Department of her hospital. She also stated that none of the other Residents were subjected to the **microaggressions** and disrespect that she endured. The Chief of her department was somewhat detached from the daily problems and the only other Black, the senior Black male physician, had little empathy for her problems. This underscores that it is unlikely that she would achieve aspects of her Desired Outcome, such as there being zero tolerance for discrimination. There was no Loss of Voice at the first level as she did have access to the Chief of the Department. There were probably allies among her fellow Residents who could be activated.

A clear opportunity for Dr. GT is the establishment of a program to emphasize behaviors that reinforce professionalism. This program could be implemented in a realistic timeframe. It would be a non-threatening dialogue to discuss the establishment of a Professional Behaviors Program with the Chief of the Department. Most members of the department are also likely to find such a program attractive. This theme of professionalism could also improve the engagement of Dr. GT, as well as others in the Department. In fact, this is an example where focusing on Inclusion behaviors could highlight the need for and produce changes in Equity.

A Better Problem to Solve would be recruiting the senior Black male physician and the Chief of the department to sponsor sessions on Professionalism in the treatment of one another and the patients. Achievement of this would move Dr. GT from being in the **Deqin-Psychologically Toxic Culture** to a low **EEQIN-Psychologically Safe Culture**.

<u>THE REFRAMED PROBLEM:</u>

The Reframed Problem is developing professional behaviors to improve patient care in the Emergency Department and developing these into a Code of Conduct for all staff in the Emergency Department.

SYSTEMIC DISCRIMINATION: CASE STUDY # 8 – AZ

DESIRED OUTCOME:

- To get the guidance I need to get my Ph.D.
- To get Prof. P.M. to review the projects and send his recommendations for further experiments.
- To be assigned to another professor during my thesis advisor's sabbatical.

SITUATION:

- I am the only Black student in the graduate chemistry program at Alexander University.
- At the end of my first year of graduate school, Prof. P. M. invited me to join his lab.
- Prof P.M. recommended that I take the Ph.D. candidacy examination, which was normally done between years 2 and 3.
- I decided to follow the advice of one of the professors on my thesis committee and postponed taking the examination.
- I passed the Ph.D. candidacy examination one semester later.
- Prof. P. M. agreed that I could use his methodology to study a biological molecule that I had selected.
- However, he did caution me that his methodology had been applied to simple organic molecules like benzene and its derivatives.
- Prof. P. M. told me that a former graduate student had a good description of an experimental system in his thesis.
- This student had a similar idea but graduated before he could test the system.

- Prof. P.M. stated that I could attempt the experiments that I envisioned if I could reconstruct the experimental system.
- I was ecstatic with this permission.
- Prof. P.M. also explained that he was more of a theoretical chemist, so would not be able to help with building the experimental apparatus.
- He would begin to guide me after I began to generate experimental data.
- I succeeded in redesigning and rebuilding the system and after about one year I began to generate reproducible experimental data.
- At about this time, Prof. P.M. left for a 1-year sabbatical.
- During his absence, I would send him the results of experiments that I had done. I prepared reports of these experiments as though they were for publication.
- Although I received acknowledgement of receipt of these reports, I never received comments on the reports nor advice on the next steps.
- This was quite frustrating and continued a pattern that I had endured during the previous 18 months in his lab.
- Often I would ask Prof. P.M. for help with a problem. He would then ask a few initial questions.
- When I began to respond, he would quickly say: 'Oh AZ, surely you know how to solve this', and that would signal the end of the session.
- I had observed, however, that my classmates would spend extended periods of time in his office getting advice on their problems.

ENVIRONMENT:

- Alexander University is a large prestigious, predominantly White institution in the Northeast of America.
- There are about 150 graduate students in the department of chemistry.

- When I entered the chemistry department, two Black students, who had both completed their Ph.D.s, were transitioning to positions in other universities.
- I became the only Black student for the next two years in the department.
- There are two Chemistry Nobel Laureates and a third professor who is considered a likely future laureate.
- He is the professor who had advised me to postpone my Ph.D. candidacy examination,
- There is one post-doctoral fellow and a total of 7 graduate students in our group. The group often has lunch together to which I have never been invited.
- Recently, one graduate student invited me to have dinner with him and his wife.
- Dinner was quite pleasant until the wife began to express her annoyance that Black undergraduate students were complaining about insensitivity and Systemic Racism.
- Earlier in the evening as we talked about jazz and our favorite old-time singers, she told me that her favorite singer was Sammy Davis Jr.
- One reason she liked Sammy Davis Jr. was that he had a White wife and never complained about being treated badly as a Black person.
- I told her, that on the contrary, Sammy Davis Jr. had participated in many marches with Dr. Martin Luther King Jr.
- I also told her that I found it inconsistent that she would have Sammy Davis Jr. as an idol and simultaneously criticize these young students.
- Since that dinner, my classmate avoids interacting with me. And I sense a greater formality when the others interact with me.
- Although the undergraduate campus is alive with the discussion of the ills of the day, graduate departments act as though they are on mountain tops, untouched by these issues.
- The chemistry department is proud of its mountain top.

- During the time that I have been a graduate student, only one other professor has ever engaged me in friendly, casual conversation.
- He is the chairperson of the chemistry department.
- I often think that he acknowledges my presence because I visit his labs to see one of his students, who is a friend of mine, and with whom I have studied together in a couple of our courses.

PROBLEM STATEMENT:

- The lack of interaction with my major thesis professor is making me unsure and anxious as to whether the experiments I am designing would lead to a Ph.D. in Physical Chemistry.

ISSUES SURROUNDING INCLUSION:

Microassaults:

- AZ suffered from a lack of support and advice.
- AZ felt that he was being set up to fail.
- AZ was shunned by lab mates after dinner with one of them.

Microinsults:

- A classmate's wife was critical of young Black students who were protesting insensitivity and racism.

Microinvalidations:

- Professor P.M. curtailed the time for guidance and help that AZ needed while giving more time to other students.
- When Professor P.M. went on sabbatical, there was no provision made for a substitute professor to guide AZ.
- Professor P.M. did not respond nor offer guidance on AZ's reports of his experiments.

ISSUES SURROUNDING EQUITY:

Privilege/Preferences:

- Professor P.M. appeared to spend more time guiding other graduate students in the group.

Processes:

- There was no simple process in place to offer advice on how to manage a difficult situation with one's Thesis Advisor.
- AZ felt that his fate rested solely in the hands of the Thesis Advisor.
- There were no periodic progress reports with entire Thesis Committee to get interim guidance.
- The current system was one where graduate students were expected to 'figure things out'.

Prospects:

- Prospects were very slim for AZ.

EQUITY-INCLUSION CULTURE MATRIX

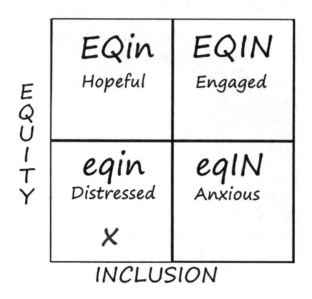

This is an example of a case where there might be an overall assumed organizational super-culture under which many cultures and subcultures exist. In a university, there can be the co-existence of the website-advertised super-culture, the culture of various schools and institutes and the subculture of departments within each School or Institute and even sub-subcultures within, for example, various labs within the department. AZ is experiencing a low Equity Culture both from the University and at the departmental level.

It is possible, that for those graduate students who have 'figured out' how to get the best out of the department processes, Equity is quite high. It is therefore more instructive for AZ to first focus on his sub-sub-culture, namely, the culture in his lab. In this lab, he is not being treated as one of the Privileged and he has not solved the 'process code' to get access and needed guidance from his Thesis Advisor. As a result, he is in a low Equity Culture. Reflection on his options along the Inclusion axis, shows that he has become mildly estranged from his lab mates, who should have been his close friends. Thus, with respect to his lab, AZ is Distressed and in a **Deqin- Psychologically Toxic Culture**.

A BETTER PROBLEM TO SOLVE:

The essence of AZ's Desired Outcome is to receive the guidance he needs to get his Ph.D. One solution was to succeed in getting his present Thesis Advisor involved, as he should be. The other is being assigned another Advisor during his Thesis Advisor's sabbatical. He does not want to change Thesis Advisors as that would most likely also involve a change in Thesis Project.

Although AZ feels alone and lost, he has opportunities, particularly with respect to the Inclusion behaviors that would stimulate engagement. One fact that is usually true of all science graduate students is their interest in discussing science. Thus, AZ could have reached out to his lab mates and asked for their comments about his experiments. He could have organized an informal lunch seminar for his group and specifically stated that he would first like to know what questions they had, and secondly, he would like to solicit their help in addressing some of the questions that he had.

In his next report to Prof. P.M. he could have included questions that were raised by his colleagues and his responses. He should copy his lab mates on this letter and also ask for Prof. P.M.'s comments and guidance on his responses, as this would be a learning experience for the entire group.

As we look along the Equity axis, AZ mentioned the one Professor who was usually cordial to him. AZ could have approached this Professor, who was one of the top professors in Physical Chemistry at Alexander University. He could have leveraged his friendship with his classmate who worked for this professor and could have asked her to arrange the meeting with her boss.

In this situation, as described, there were opportunities for others to help AZ recover from his own Loss of Voice. They were potential allies. In addition, the timeframe for a 'Hopeful Plan to Endure the

Pain', combined with effective dampening of the effects of Loss of Voice, could have moved AZ into an **AeqIN-Psychologically Unsafe Culture**, if not better.

THE REFRAMED PROBLEM:

The Reframed Problem becomes focused on methods of receiving guidance when one's Thesis Advisor is missing in action. AZ should address the problem of getting input on his experiments, first from his lab mates, and second from the sympathetic professor. He should send the results of these interactions to his Thesis Advisor and ask for his further guidance. If both of these succeeded, this would move AZ from the **Deqin-Psychologically Toxic Culture** to at least the **AeqIN-Psychologically Unsafe Culture**, because he would quite likely be able to continue to engage his lab mates and even make the lunch sessions one way to manage when a professor leaves for an extended Sabbatical.

SYSTEMIC DISCRIMINATION: CASE STUDY # 9 – DL

DESIRED OUTCOME:

- Advance to Vice President (VP).

SITUATION:

- I was a Director of R&D of my previous company for 13 years.
- I began as an entry-level engineer and was promoted to manager after 7 years and to Director of R&D after another 7 years.
- My performances as Director were mostly 'exceeds Expectations'.
- I had a great relationship with my boss, who was a VP, and who tried to be my mentor.
- Mentorship was very important in order to be assigned the types of projects that involved the entire organization and made one visible to other VPs.
- I was assigned one of the projects that lasted 1 1/2 years. It increased my visibility to all the VPs and was deemed very successful.
- My VP/Mentor was quite pleased with my performance. Nonetheless, I was not offered a second assignment.
- Although the processes for assignment selection and promotion to VP were not transparent, individuals who were promoted to VP had received repeat assignments.
- I had several career development discussions, but was never told what I needed to do to advance to the VP level.
- I participated in the usual courses and training for managers.
- Of interest, my initial assessment indicated that I would receive 'at least two promotions'.

- It seemed prophetic in that I had received two promotions and no more.
- During this time, one woman with project management experience but no R&D expertise was promoted to VP of R&D.
- Although I was quite frustrated by the lack of useful advice on what I needed in order to be promoted to the VP level, I remained reluctant to aggressively promote my achievements and candidacy.
- At the next merger, I took the opportunity to leave and join another company.

ENVIRONMENT:

- The company was a global company with 2000 employees.
- Most of the VPs were White males.
- Similarly, most of the entry engineers were White males who were recruited from the same set of universities.
- Of interest, however, there was more diversity at the Director level, but those promoted to VP level were primarily Caucasians.
- There was little transparency around selection for global, cross departmental assignments or promotion to the VP level.
- Mentorship and advocacy from senior executives seemed to be essential for significant promotions.
- Human Resources (HR) was primarily concerned with hiring, salary and merit increase management and reductions in force.
- HR was neither decision maker nor influencer when it pertained to career growth.

PROBLEM STATEMENT:

- There is no transparent assessment of potential and career development.

ISSUES SURROUNDING INCLUSION:

Microassaults:

- There are no reported **microassaults.**

Microinsults:

- There are no reported **microinsults.**

Microinvalidations:

- DL did not receive a second special assignment which was a common occurrence before promotion to VP Level.
- DL's perception was that the initial assessment limited him to two promotions, despite his 'Exceeds Expectations' performances.
- DL received no further advancement after being a Director for 13 years.
- DL participated in several career development discussions but was given no information about steps needed to advance to the VP level.

ISSUES SURROUNDING EQUITY:

Privilege/Preferences:

- VP positions seemed to be reserved for White males.

Processes:

- DL had a very supportive mentor.
- Criteria for selection for second cross-department assignments were not clear.
- Career Development sessions did not address what was needed for promotion to VP.

Prospects:

- The lack of success in receiving a second assignment suggested further advancement was not likely.

EQUITY-INCLUSION CULTURE MATRIX

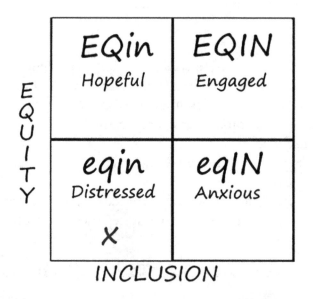

The Equity axis reveals a significant problem when Privilege and Processes work together to exclude full participation. At the VP Level, Privilege for White males existed. Processes for selection were opaque and DL's Prospects in the company seemed to have reached its pinnacle. The reason why DL never received a second assignment was never explained to him. The selection criteria for a second assignment remained a closely held secret.

At the department level, Inclusion behaviors were practiced and individuals were motivated. However, above the Director Level, for DL, Inclusion was lacking. DL was a Director for 13 years and had continued to receive 'Exceeds Expectations' for his performance evaluations. This might suggest possibilities for DL to improve his situation by creation of a better Culture.

DL is in a **Deqin-Psychologically Toxic Culture**, in which Equity and Inclusion for him are both low. In such a situation we often recommend the individual consider leaving the organization, if possible.

However, as mentioned above, given the positive view his boss has of his performance, there might be opportunities to improve his situation in Inclusion and move to the **AeqIN-Psychologically Unsafe Culture**.

DL does not have Loss of Voice at the first level as he continued to question why he had not received a second multidepartment assignment, which seemed to be a prerequisite for promotion to the VP position in R&D. It appears that there was Loss of Voice at the second level as there were no obvious allies, apart from his mentor, to speak on DL's behalf. There was Loss of Voice at the third level as Human Resources did not play an active role in counseling employees. In fact, there seemed to have been a cynical culture in which one received several career development sessions without ever being told what one needed to do to develop one's career.

DL was slow to build a 'Hopeful Plan to Endure the Pain'.

A BETTER PROBLEM TO SOLVE:

DL identifies lack of a transparent assessment for potential and career development as the key problem. An assessment for potential existed early in DL's career with the company but seemed to have been used as a single predictive event. A similar assessment for further career opportunities for those at the Director level could be offered. Although seeking to solve this as a problem might not result in DL advancing to a VP of R&D, this assessment could be achieved in a realistic time frame and could potentially benefit many others. In addition, the dialogue between DL and his supervisor and mentor could be conducted in a non-threatening manner. The request for a formal assessment designed for mid-career employees could increase the motivation and hence engagement of these employees. It could also improve retention of these high performers. Both Equity and Inclusion for the Directors could improve.

A formal assessment for mid-career employees, who desire it, coupled with a discussion of potential career opportunities in the company could only be positive for the employee and the company. As an experienced Director, DL could develop allies by discussing this approach with other

Directors. With this approach, DL, as an experienced and seemingly valued Director of the company, would be taking a positive step in managing his career and potentially improving the career paths for other Directors.

THE REFRAMED PROBLEM:

DL should determine whether he is open to a VP position in departments other than R&D. If he is, DL should take the personal responsibility to explore whether there are other opportunities in the company where his expertise and experience as a leader could be used. This might require a change in career path. He should do this simultaneously with his push for establishment of a transparent Mid-Career Assessment. Should DL do this, he would be working to increase his Prospects and improve Processes in the company. By increasing these two aspects of Equity, he would be moving up in the **Deqin-Psychologically Toxic Culture** towards the **HEQin-Psychologically Unsafe, Hopeful Culture**. DL might even have created an **EEQIN-Psychologically Safe Culture!** DL would have contributed to improving Equity for mid-level managers in his company.

The Reframed Problem is creation of Assessment and Counseling for Mid-Career employees and identification of opportunities in other departments that could lead to a VP position in his company.

If DL were not willing to transition from R&D, his moving to another company made sense. Hopefully, his new company is stronger in Equity and one where his contributions to fostering Inclusion would be welcome.

SYSTEMIC DISCRIMINATION: CASE STUDY # 10 – RH

DESIRED OUTCOME:

- To receive a long overdue promotion.

SITUATION:

- I am a Black female with a Ph.D. in the Social Sciences and have been working with a government agency for over 20 years.
- I have been passed over several times for promotions.
- The explanation has always been that they had chosen a candidate from outside the company.
- I have applied for several different positions for which I was qualified.
- I have completed many training programs, including CDC certifications, County and State programs, as well as consultant training.
- Every time an external candidate is hired, I have to train that new hire for the position that I was denied.
- A few years ago, the departments changed from being primarily White to primarily Black: West Indians, Africans and African Americans.
- Foreign born Blacks were discriminated against more than African Americans.
- After many unsuccessful interviews, the union recommended that I take courses in interviewing skills and resume writing. I did this for two years in a row.
- Finally, after 18 years of no recourse, I filed a grievance against the organization.

- Review of my several interviews by the shop steward revealed the following conclusion.
- The conclusion was that given my tenure as President of the Union and my length of service, promotion into higher management would create a conflict. It would also increase my salary above the mean for the job I was seeking.
- 'In order not to allow these problems to take away the joy of the day', I used EAP to get help to:
  o Control my anger;
  o Control negative feelings;
  o Work on my analytical skills;
  o Work on self-help approaches;
  o Learn how to ask questions in a non-threatening manner; and
  o Learn not to take things personally.

ENVIRONMENT:

- The environment was toxic. One had to be part of the clique, and if not liked, no one 'pushed you forward'.
- Mobility was not assured and ways to progress were unclear.
- The rules, regulations and guidelines were observed to varying degrees, and depended on the particular manager.
- Occasionally, the Union evaluated adherence to Binding Employee Contracts.
- It was not uncommon that when supervisors were asked to fill middle manager positions, they were not compensated appropriately.
- It was also not uncommon that when there were vacancies for higher positions, the same few individuals would be detailed to those open slots for experience.
- Selection for experience in open slots depended on whether one was liked by the superior.
- Although the organization is now predominantly Black, senior positions are invariably filled by external White candidates.
- West Indian and African Black employees endure and persevere in the environment much longer than other groups.

- One internal White employee was recently passed over for promotion when her mentor left the organization.
- Whereas the Whites seem to help each other, such support for each other is lacking among the Black groups.
- Many Black professionals are leaving in frustration.

PROBLEM STATEMENT:

- Lack of Equity and unfair practices against minorities are common.

ISSUES SURROUNDING INCLUSION:

Microassaults:

- RH felt the need to take many self-help courses.
- RH had to train external hires for position she was denied.
- Credit taken for others' Performance.
- The Union President Position and years of service prevented her from becoming a manager.
- Required to take classes in resume writing and interviewing.

Microinsults:

- Foreign Black employees encountered more discrimination compared to their American counterparts.
- Employees are predominantly Black, but Whites fill leadership roles.
- RH's promotion would place her salary above the median for the job.

Microinvalidations:

- Candidates for advanced positions were always chosen from outside the organization.
- RH has a Ph.D. but could not obtain promotion.
- Candidates from the outside were preferred for higher positions.
- RH was told to learn how to ask questions in a non-threatening manner.

<u>ISSUES SURROUNDING EQUITY:</u>

<u>Privilege/Preferences:</u>

- Blacks were excluded from, while Whites were placed in positions of leadership.
- Those employees who were part of a clique were preferentially advanced.

<u>Processes:</u>

- There were no established HR processes.
- No mechanism was available for Aggrieved individuals to discuss concerns.
- Rules and regulations were inconsistently implemented.
- There was a lack of appropriate compensation for employees.
- Processes for advancement were not transparent.

<u>Prospects:</u>

- Prospects for RH's advancement seem nonexistent.
- Many Black professionals leave the organization in frustration.
- RH had many unsuccessful interviews.
- RH completed CDC certifications and many training programs.
- RH filed a grievance after 18 years of being passed over for promotions.

EQUITY – INCLUSION CULTURE MATRIX

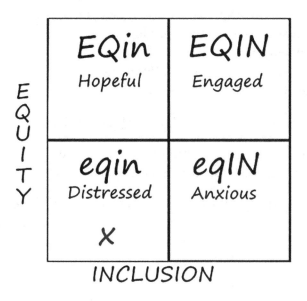

RH is in a **Deqin-Psychologically Toxic Culture**. She is so distressed that 'in order not to allow these problems to take away the joy of the day' she reached out to EAP and took courses for control of anger and negative feelings. Perhaps, very revealing was also that RH took courses in learning how to ask questions in a non-threatening way. The status of Inclusion reeks of **microaggressions** and inability to be one's authentic self. There is no attempt nor pretense at Equity. A preference for White leaders and particularly external White hires; the presence of favored groups or cliques; and no transparent processes for advancement, conspire with the lack of inclusion behaviors to create a **Deqin-Psychologically Toxic Culture**.

One of the roles of the union, via the grievance process, is to challenge management as employees are adversely affected by the absence of effective Equity rules and regulations. However, the union has not addressed Inclusion behaviors among the employees. The obvious sense of competing factions among foreign-born Blacks and US-born Blacks is palpable in this case.

RH did not experience Loss of Voice because she represented herself diligently in her pursuit of her goal. Loss of Voice at the second level was also preserved in that the Union did discuss her case with management. There was Loss of Voice at the third level, however, because the appeal process to management, who made final decisions, seemed opaque and impenetrable. RH did not have a 'Hopeful Plan to Endure the Pain', except to keep fighting!

A BETTER PROBLEM TO SOLVE:

RH'S Desired Outcome to receive 'a long overdue promotion' is a decision that is made by senior management.

As we look at the Equity – Inclusion Culture Matrix, there is little that RH can do to increase Equity in the organization because this is the responsibility of senior management. There is, however, something that RH can do on the Inclusion axis.

Inclusion emphasizes the behaviors that help employees treat each other with respect and exploits their unique views and contributions. This increases the engagement and productivity of both the employees and the department. As President of the Union, she has the opportunity to make the case, to the unionized workers, of the importance of including everyone.

If RH were to focus on improving Inclusion in the department, she would be working on an issue that would benefit both the co-workers and the entire department. Given the dedicated effort that RH expended in improving her academic, professional, and personal leadership capabilities, it is probably a wonderful opportunity to initiate a much-needed program on Inclusion behaviors. Success in establishing this program and demonstrating improvement in the support of Black employees for one another, along with improvement in productivity, would be a powerful addition to her resume. This addition could impress those who are responsible for making decisions on promotion that RH is a talented manager.

The Better Problem to Solve is the development and implementation of a program to improve Inclusion behaviors in the department.

THE REFRAMED PROBLEM:

RH should reframe her approach to achieving her desire to receive a promotion. She should focus on collaboration among her unionized co-workers by introducing behaviors that improve Inclusion and consequently, the engagement and productivity of the department. Increase in the productivity of the department would be a visible demonstration of her capabilities.

SYSTEMIC DISCRIMINATION: CASE STUDY # 11 – CF

DESIRED OUTCOME:

- Be promoted to the Manager position in which I had acted for 10 months.

SITUATION:

- I have worked in this housing agency for 20 years as a Community Development Assistant.
- About 12 months ago, the Manager of the group abruptly departed the agency and I was placed in the position as Acting Manager.
- At that time, I was in a position that was three levels below that of the Manager position.
- There were about 4-5 people in our group of 50 people who were in positions higher than mine.
- I think I was asked to step into the role of Manager for 90 days because the senior manager liked that I was industrious and well organized.
- Assignment was extended from 90 days to 6 months and finally to 10 months.
- During my time at the agency, I took many personal development courses; volunteered to work on team projects outside of my direct responsibility; and offered to develop presentations because of my excellent writing skills.
- I followed the advice of a former Mentor who told me: 'Do not stifle your ambition'.
- At the time of being asked to act as Manager, I was 12 hours short of completing my B.A. degree.

- During the time I acted as Manager, the group met all Performance Metrics and all major projects were completed on time.
- This was a particular challenge because the office had to be closed due to COVID-19 restrictions and I had to manage people and an $80 million budget, virtually.
- The Manager position was advertised externally and I applied for it a few times as I worked on improving my resume.
- This included documenting my various contributions and achievements more clearly, as advised by Human Resources, and completing my B.A.
- The requirements for the Manager job were a Masters or a Bachelor's degree with significant experience.
- After 10 months, an external candidate with a Masters degree and some experience in another agency was hired.
- I was asked to support him as he 'got his sea legs', which I did. Two months later he hired a woman who had worked with him as his deputy.
- I felt really defeated.
- I appealed because, not only had I applied for this Manager's position, but also for other senior positions that were higher than my position.
- Finally, I was promoted to a position two levels higher than my base position.
- I was happy because many of my colleagues cheered when my promotion was announced.
- I have started a graduate program.

ENVIRONMENT:

- The Agency has 100 employees and two groups.
- Each of the two groups has a Human Resources (HR) representative that reports to a larger HR group that supports several Agencies.
- HR representatives focus more on administrative functions, such as time sheets, hiring and compensation.

- There is no cultivation of leadership, nor grooming of individuals.
- Employees have to be responsible for their own growth and need to take personal initiative in order to advance.
- However, if you are too aggressive, that might be a negative. For example, on occasion people would comment about me: "why is she in everything?"
- There is preference for hiring external candidates for the Manager and Senior Manager positions.
- New leadership is discussing training opportunities.
- You are allowed to volunteer on teams outside your area; to create special projects to address identified gaps; and to interact with external agencies, all on your own initiative.

PROBLEM STATEMENT:

- Cronyism is rampant in this organization.
- Each new external leader brings their own people without regard for the internal employees who have contributed to the company.

ISSUES SURROUNDING INCLUSION:

Microassaults:

- Twice, CF trained other employees for positions for which she had applied.
- CF was denied the Manager position after acting for 10 months under challenging conditions. She had to organize and manage a remote - working team because of COVID-19. She completed all projects on time and on budget.
- Despite her excellent performance as acting Manager and despite the fact that her assignment was extended from 3 months to 10 months, CF was not offered the position.
- CF remained employed for 20 years without a promotion.
- CF was criticized for taking on too many projects.

Microinsults:

- No **microinsults** were reported.

Microinvalidations:

- A White manager was hired after CF had acted as manager for 10 months.
- CF was finally promoted to a position two levels above her previous position but below Manager-level position that she had held for 10 months.
- CF was frequently passed over for positions for which she had applied.
- There was a continual lack of recognition of CF's contributions to teams outside of her own area.

ISSUES SURROUNDING EQUITY:

Privilege/Preferences:
- There was a preference for hiring external managers who frequently hired external deputies.
- White employees had been promoted to manager without having a degree.

Processes:

- CF was finally promoted to a position two levels above previous position but below the Manager-level position that she held for 10 months.
- CF was self-motivated, took courses to improve herself, helped teams outside her own area, and was periodically ridiculed for being too 'ambitious'.
- There was no formal training or coaching programs in the organization.
- CF was at the same level after 20 years.
- Little was done for the psychological health of the employees.
- The agency serviced the community and as a result the poor morale of employees affected their service to the community.
- There were frequent changes in leadership.

- Human Resources organization was not engaged.
- There seemed to be a poor organizational structure.
- Meritocracy was measured by 'time in place', time in a position.
- The Public, the external customer was not a focus of the organization.
- There were no standardized protocols for promotion and advancement.
- There were no development programs nor was there succession planning.
- Middle managers were not incentivized to build and promote internal talent.

Prospects:

- CF worked tirelessly on improving her capabilities but was unsuccessful in securing a promotion.
- Personal initiative and enthusiasm, although necessary for success, was also viewed negatively.
- She was encouraged to take on additional projects and 'not stifle her ambition.'
- Her promotion came only after she made a formal complaint based on the fact that she had performed with distinction as a Manager for 10 months and could not secure a promotion.
- Leaders recognized her abilities and turned to her to take on a Manager's role in an emergency.
- There was a high turnover in the organization as individuals, who were frustrated with the lack of advancement or career prospects, departed.

EQUITY INCLUSION CULTURE MATRIX

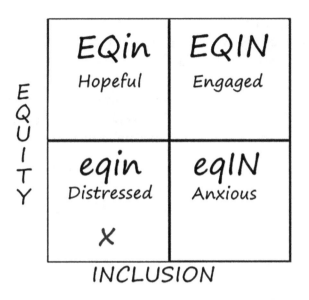

The absence of robust and transparent processes that govern employee evaluation, promotion, and expectations in the organization has created a psychologically unsafe culture. This culture has bred poor employee motivation, low performance expectations, lack of pride in performance and criticism of other employees who are enthusiastic and self-motivated. There was high turnover, which is a characteristic of **Deqin** cultures. The preference to hire middle managers from outside the organization devalued the present work force and gave them few prospects for advancement in their careers. The result was a low Equity Culture.

The frequent **microinvalidations** by denying CF's applications for promotions, despite her diligence and extra work to contribute to projects and to help other teams, makes one wonder at her emotional and psychological strength. In addition, the **microinvalidation** of having her train individuals who had been appointed to positions for which she had applied reveal a certain lack of concern for employees.

Generally, Inclusion behaviors are low in this Culture. CF is in a **Deqin -Psychologically Toxic Culture**.

CF did not have Loss of Voice at the first level as she continued to apply for positions for which she was qualified. Her appointment to substitute in a position three levels above her level, suggests that Loss of Voice at the second level was not fully present, in that she had a powerful ally in at least one manager. However, there was no effective organizational process to deal with Loss of Voice at the third level. CF had no 'Hopeful Plan to Endure the Pain', which was remarkable.

It should also be noted that 'new leadership is discussing training opportunities.' This will begin to improve Equity. It would also demonstrate the importance of actions of senior leadership with respect to Equity.

A BETTER PROBLEM TO SOLVE:

CF's Desired Outcome was to be promoted to a Manager level equivalent to the one for which she had served as substitute manager for 10 months. CF would also like to address the problem of the Preference for external hires for the Manager positions. Given the severe lack of Equity in Processes, without a major change in leadership, it is unlikely that either her Desired Outcome goals could be achieved or her Problem Statement resolved in a reasonable timeframe. The Prospects for CF, however, are good.

CF had not only fulfilled one measure of meritocracy in this organization, namely 'time in place', CF had also demonstrated her leadership and technical capabilities. She had met a second measure that could not be overlooked, namely, Performance. CF led the team to complete all projects on time and on budget, while managing in an unprecedented situation that was caused by the COVID Pandemic. This justified the judgment and confidence of whomever made the unusual decision to select and elevate her to take on the Acting Manager position. This was further validated in that they extended this assignment from an initial 3 months to 10 months.

Thus, a Better Problem to Solve is the one that was associated with CF's persistence to achieve her Desired Outcome. She was promoted to one level below the Manager level. This made her Prospects quite positive. CF has now personally moved from **Deqin-Psychologically Toxic Culture** to the low area of **HEQin-Hopeful Psychologically Unsafe Culture**. This might give hope to others that their efforts might eventually be recognized and rewarded. It presents an opportunity to address a problem that would realistically benefit other employees. It could also benefit the organization by increasing Individual Engagement and improving retention.

Thus, a Better Problem to Solve is developing systems for recognizing and rewarding employees who perform beyond expectations. CF has, as allies, the manager who promoted her as well as other employees who were deserving of promotion. Her promotion has also increased her Voice.

THE REFRAMED PROBLEM:

CF should approach the manager, who had acted as a mentor, and who had made the courageous decision to put her temporarily in the Manager's role, with the following proposal: development of a process to identify top-performing individuals, particularly those who have been in their positions a long time, for rapid promotion or elevation to positions with increased responsibility.

SYSTEMIC DISCRIMINATION: CASE STUDY # 12 – OS

DESIRED OUTCOME:

- To be treated fairly.
- Improvement of attitudes in the Organization.

SITUATION:

- I am an MBA with an undergraduate major in Accounting and am a Certified Fraud Examiner.
- I was a Senior Corporate Auditor for a large Bank in City X.
- However, I did not see a clear path for advancement.
- There were 40-50 auditors.
- Auditors have great visibility, become experts in the respective audit area and often ascend to Officer / Manager positions such as Loan Officer, Fiscal Officer, Trust Officer, etc. However, these positions seemed to go primarily to White auditors.
- I applied for an Assistant Manager of Accounting position in a Federal Reserve Bank (FRB).
- The Federal Reserve Bank (12 District Banks) is the Central Banking system of the United States and controls its money supply. The Bank runs like a well-oiled machine.
- There were no Black Executives in the Federal Reserve Bank.
- There were two finalists for the position, a White Female (WF) and I. WF was hired as Assistant Manager of Accounting. WF had been Assistant Manager of Accounting at a Bank and had only a Bachelor of Science degree, and no Certification.
- I was offered a staff position in Disaster Recovery and Data Security because I had experience in internal controls to mitigate Risk.

- Data Security controlled who had access to classified documents and as a result was a critical position that provided a lot of visibility.
- Whereas I reported directly to the VP of Accounting and dotted line to the Manager of Accounting, WF reported to the Manager of Accounting, who reported to the VP of Accounting.
- For about two years, I had received 'Far Exceeds' evaluations from the VP. One day, without much discussion, the VP told me that because he was overwhelmed, I would be reporting to WF.
- WF went on maternity leave for two months.
- On her return she complained that she was surprised that I had never called her during those two months and now questioned how I had been spending my time at work.
- I had prepared a detailed Disaster Recovery Plan, for example, for the accounting department, including a test plan for evacuation, accounting computer systems, backup systems, personnel available to bring systems up, drills, recording, time etc.
- I gave the Disaster Recovery Plan to the Manager of Accounting, He showed it to WF, and he made an issue that I had shown the preparedness of one (1) process on one (1) page of an approximate 25-page report as 99.9% rather than 100 %.
- The Accounting Manager had the report for about two weeks prior to WF returning from maternity leave and had not brought this to my attention.
- The VP of Accounting informed me that hence forth, all my work had to go through WF who was now responsible for preparing my performance evaluations.
- WF informed me that I was to document my work activities in 15 minute-intervals and submit it to her weekly. I prepared this document as requested.
- I felt helpless and very stressed as I didn't understand why this was happening.
- WF and the Manager of Accounting began to make working at the Bank unpleasant for me.

- Headquarters asked for feedback on a report. Normally the computer associates would respond to such requests. However, I was told to lead / coordinate a response to the report and work with two computer associates.
- The two White computer associates expressed no interest in offering a response (they had not read the report).
- I stated that I had read the report and would send my thoughts in a report to them for edit and approval before forwarding to Headquarters. (All three of us would have been reported as authors on the report).
- While I was writing the response, the White computer associates complained to WF that I had worked on it even though they thought there should be no response. WF agreed with the computer associates, and this carried forward as a negative on my performance appraisal.
- The worst situation occurred when the VP asked me to perform a bank-wide research project on Disaster Recovery and submit three weeks later. I researched the topic, interviewed managers, and executives, and completed a written report with illustrative graphs and gave it to WF for review and edit - five days before the deadline.
- After getting no feedback from WF, I asked WF, on the date the report was due, whether she had submitted the report and she told me that she had to redo it.
- She showed me a report that was poorly written, had no paragraphs nor structure and fell short of the high quality of my report.
- Three to four days later, the VP called me into his office. He was very angry. His face was flushed and he blamed me for turning in the report late.
- I explained what had occurred and offered to show him my evidential records of the report and date / time it was submitted to WF.
- VP started ranting and raving and said that he believed WF and did not want to see my records (report with date / time and work activity documentation (as required by WF) because

if she had held on to the report as I claimed, it would mean that she was crazy!

- He said that I was a liar and if I said one more thing concerning WF in the meeting, he would fire me on the spot!
- With this and other racist episodes, I realized that the entire management line from Asst. Manager to Manager to VP were aligned in their mission to force me to leave the Bank.
- On one occasion, I had appealed to Human Resources (HR) regarding time due me (but denied) for working on a Disaster Recovery test on a weekend.
- No sooner had I returned to my desk, I received word that my visit to HR had been reported to the VP. The HR department reported to an Executive who ultimately reported to the VP described above.
- Shortly, thereafter the bank had its first layoff. I and a Jewish male were terminated.
- I filed a work-related discrimination and wrongful termination suit with the Equal Employment Opportunity Commission (EEOC).
- The EEOC performed an investigation and concluded that they could not find ample evidence of discrimination. EEOC only interviewed members of the Accounting Department, so it was no surprise that they said that they had found no evidence of discrimination.
- Approximately one month after I received notice of the EEOC findings, I received a phone call from a Black employee at the Bank.
- She informed me that the VP of Accounting had called a meeting of all employees in the Bank and among other Bank news, reported (bragged) that under his auspices, the 'Bank had never lost an EEOC case.'
- She felt this was a direct reference to my situation.

ENVIRONMENT:

- There were approx. 250 employees in the Bank with a total of 15 to 20 Blacks.

- My unit had 20 Whites and 3 Blacks.
- Blacks did not feel welcomed and in the cafeteria had to avoid sitting together as sitting with Whites was clearly preferred.
- A young Black graduate was hired but did not last long. He made the fatal error of following the best practice advice of his Mentor and contested his negative performance evaluation.
- HR focused primarily on administrative issues, such as payroll, hiring etc.
- When employees had concerns, they frequently looked to the VP of their section for help, and not HR.
- Although the Data Security aspect of my job was well received by the various departments, there was not a similar embrace for Disaster Recovery analyses and planning.

PROBLEM STATEMENT:

- I worked in an organization in which I could not get an explanation of the decisions that were being made against me.

ISSUES SURROUNDING INCLUSION:

Microassaults:

- The sudden change in the attitude of the VP, who threatened to fire OS if she suggested that WF was lying, was a tremendous and unexpected blow.
- OS was called a Liar by the VP.
- OS was summarily told to report to WF, after having received 'Far Exceeds' evaluations for two years from the VP.
- OS had to report her activities in 15-minute increments to WF, now her supervisor. This was done out of resentment and to establish control. This bordered on harassment.
- OS' colleagues complained that she was unnecessarily working on the assignment from Headquarters, on which they had refused to collaborate.

Microinsults:

- Black employees were strongly discouraged from sitting together at lunch.

Microinvalidations:

- OS' expertise was denied - her report on Disaster Recovery for the Accounting Department was dismissed.
- OS had to report to her supervisor every 15 minutes. This was used by the supervisor to establish control over OS.
- The VP's excuse that he was too busy to supervise her and that she should report to the Assistant Accounting Manager was, in effect, a two-level demotion.
- The decision not to consider her response to the request from Headquarters did not value her professionalism.

ISSUES SURROUNDING EQUITY:

Privilege/Preferences:

- Office/Manager positions, such a Loan Officer, Fiscal Officer, went to White auditors.
- The award of the job to a White female with lower achievements revealed preference for White candidates.
- The 'environment' was silently hostile to Blacks and made it clear that it was preferred that Blacks not sit together in the cafeteria.

Processes:

- The reason for the change from her reporting to the VP to reporting to the White Female was not sufficiently explained.
- There was no mechanism for OS to report her concern confidentially. The VP was immediately made aware of her visit to HR.
- HR was not evaluating issues independent of the heads of departments.

- It was astounding that OS was punished for responding to a request from Headquarters.

Prospects:

- OS was summarily told to report to the WF, who was less qualified than she was, and had gotten the job for which they were both applicants.
- Initially she reported directly to the VP and dotted line to the Accounting Manager, to whom WF reported. The Accounting Manager reported to the VP. This change in her reporting relationship was two levels lower than her initial position.
- WF had a hostile attitude to OS and did not accept her work.
- The general lack of support for Disaster Recovery assessment and activities devalued one major part of her job.
- No opportunity was made to find her another position or department where her expertise in Data Security could be used.

EQUITY INCLUSION CULTURE MATRIX

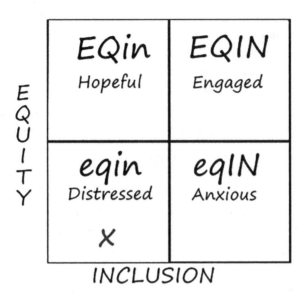

Equity in this Bank was low, including during the first two years of her employment when OS received 'Far Exceeds' evaluations from the VP. Privilege was present and HR Processes were not apparent. Inclusion was also generally low as the few Blacks who worked there could not be their authentic selves and were discouraged from sitting together at lunch. In the first two years, Inclusion was strong for OS. Her expertise was recognized, and for this she felt valued. Initially, OS was in an **AeqIN-Psychologically Unsafe Culture**. Her anxiety level was high, because, although initially she had significant support and positive Inclusion behaviors from her boss, the VP, Equity overall was low. The culture changed to **Deqin-Psychologically Toxic Culture** when the VP demoted her and she had to report to WF.

The sudden, unexplained, two-level demotion seemed arbitrary. The lack of transparency, and accountability for decision-making in the organization made it difficult for OS to understand or accept the change in her reporting relationship. The refusal of the VP to look at OS' documentation of the Disaster Recovery plan and her completion dates was at best bizarre. There was also no clear explanation as to why her Disaster-Recovery Plan was not acceptable. These issues of Privilege and lack of Processes, combined with abysmal Prospects for OS, meant that Equity was extremely low. OS had progressed from anxiety to being deeply distressed. OS had already experienced total Loss of Voice when the VP changed her reporting relationship from himself to a person two levels below him and there was no effective organizational process to address the issue. It appears that OS had not developed a 'Hopeful Plan to Endure the Pain' when she was demoted.

A BETTER PROBLEM TO SOLVE:

OS' Desired Outcome that required improvement of 'attitudes in the organization' and addressing the problem of lack of transparency in decision-making was unlikely to be realized in a short timeframe. The tension between OS and WF did not allow an easy dialogue and the relationship between OS and the VP, her former boss, had deteriorated without explanation. However, before filing a complaint with EEOC, OS could have leveraged the two years of 'Far Exceeds' evaluations from the VP, which she had received when she had reported directly to him. She could have asked the following questions:

- Why am I being treated differently?
- What are the things I've done right and what are the things I've done wrong?
- When did your assessment of me change?
- Why did you not want to see the proof of the report I had?
- If my performance is not up to standards what can I do to improve?
- If I were White would you have treated me the same way?
- Could I report to the Accounting Manager, instead?
- Is there an opportunity to move to another department where I can focus on Data Security?

If the VP refused a face-to-face meeting, she could have sent it to him by email. A decision to involve EEOC implies that one is, in effect, prepared to leave the organization. Therefore, there would have been no disadvantage in asking these questions.

THE REFRAMED PROBLEM:

Depending on the answer to the above questions, OS could have asked for an audit of the two Disaster-Recovery plans that she had created and a transfer to a different unit to focus on Data Security. However, since overall Equity is low in this Bank and the Environment is not welcoming to Blacks, our Reframed Problem would be to resign from this organization and find a job in a psychologically safer culture.

SYSTEMIC DISCRIMINATION: CASE STUDY # 13 – BV

DESIRED OUTCOME:

- I would like to see more diversity in my company.
- I want my company to hire another Black person. (several Black employees).
- I want to be considered for a promotion under the same terms as my White colleagues.

SITUATION:

- I am a Black female sales executive for a fortune 500 company and I have worked at this company for the past five years.
- I am the only Black person in my sales region.
- I earn a six-figure income.
- I have always received excellent employee evaluations.
- I have received a merit increase every year.
- I have referred several Black candidates for open positions, but none was hired.
- My opinions are not valued in meetings, but other people steal all my ideas.
- My boss has recommended that I apply for the two-year Sales Manager Training Program. I declined because the Product Manager role gives more responsibility, visibility and potential for further advancement.

ENVIRONMENT:

- I get along with all my co-workers and manager.
- My manager likes and respects me.

- I am frequently assigned additional projects because the manager knows she can count on me.
- My manager has asked me to apply for the manager's training program. This is a two - year program.
- I have no desire to be a Sales Manager but would like to be a Product Manager.
- The company says one has to be a Sales Manager to be considered for a Product Manager position.
- I have seen several of my White colleagues get promoted without going through the two-year Sales Manager training program.

PROBLEM STATEMENT:

- ABC company has given me excellent evaluations and raises every year but denies me the promotion that I want. I complain that there is not enough diversity in the company. I am the only Black person in my region, and there are no Black managers in the company.

ISSUES OF INCLUSION:

Microassaults:

- BV's opinions are not valued in meetings.
- BV's colleagues get credit for her ideas.

Microinsults:

- BV's company ignored her recommendations to hire Blacks.

Microinvalidations:

- BV's Manager recommended she apply for the Sales Manager instead of Product Manager Training Program.
- Despite BV's excellent performance evaluations, she does not receive an exception from the two-year Sales Manager Training requirement.

ISSUES SURROUNDING EQUITY:

Privilege/Preferences:

- Preference is given to some White employees in that the requirement of completing a two-year Sales Manager training program is waived in their promotion to Product Manager.

Processes:

- There is a lack of transparency in how exceptions for the two-year Sales Manager Training Program requirement are made.

Prospects:

- BV fears that if she takes the two-year Sales Manager Training Program, she might lose any opportunity to get the Product Manager position.
- The lack of commitment to hiring Black managers, including candidates identified by BV causes her to be skeptical that taking the Sales Manager training would result in her becoming a Product Manager.

EQUITY-INCLUSION CULTURE MATRIX

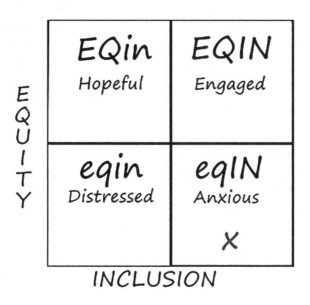

The preference given to some White employees by allowing them to skip the two-year Sales Manager training requirement, and the lack of transparency in the decision-making process suggest defects in Equity. In addition, BV's prospects in the company are questionable. Since there are no Black managers, she fears that she might not become a Sales Manager even after taking the Sales Manager Training Program.

Inclusion at the level of BV's department is quite strong. However, Inclusion at the company level is weak. BV is in the **AeqIN- Anxious, Psychologically Unsafe Culture** quadrant. In effect, BV had no Loss of Voice and because she was satisfied overall with her job, she had not created a 'Hopeful Plan to Endure the Pain'.

A BETTER PROBLEM TO SOLVE:

BV's Desired Outcome for an increase in the number of Blacks and diversity in the company is unlikely to be achievable in a short timeframe, given the present history of ABC company. Her desire to be promoted under the same criteria as her privileged White counterparts is a Desired Outcome that might recruit allies. The realization of this desire could occur in a reasonable timeframe. She has had a direct dialogue with her boss about the issue. The fact that the boss recommends that BV take the Sales Manager Training Program suggests that she does not believe that BV would win the battle of getting selected for the Product Manager Training Program. BV has a good relationship with her boss and her colleagues. Therefore, her best course of action is to work in the Inclusion area of Influence.

It is quite likely that there are others in the company who are perturbed by the preference being given to some employees with respect to the requirements for becoming a Product Manager. These are potential allies. BV and these allies should identify sympathetic managers and seek their advice on the best ways to make the criteria for exceptions transparent. BV could start by seeking her manager's support in this effort. The simple rationale should be focused on changing a system that is causing some employees to become less engaged.

The Better Problem to Solve is establishing more transparency and clear criteria for exceptions to the prerequisites needed to gain entrance to the Product Manager Training Program.

THE REFRAMED PROBLEM:

BV should recruit her manager as an ally in her push for transparency and fairness in the selection of Product Managers. Since BV says she is fully engaged and likes the company, it is clear that building allies is a better strategy than creating an adversarial relationship to achieve her Desired Outcome. Individual Engagement is critical for the success of managing products. It is unlikely that senior management would risk having several managers lose motivation and become less engaged.

SYSTEMIC DISCRIMINATION: CASE STUDY # 14 – VM

DESIRED OUTCOME:

- To be transferred and promoted to the position of Tech Operations Site Head in one of the major countries.

SITUATION:

- In 1985 I was hired in Quality control of a leading international company with its headquarters in Europe.
- One year later, I transferred to the Technical Operations Department.
- Because of the market size and importance of the FDA, the US Tech Operations (Tech Ops.) Organization was strategically very important for the successful manufacture and launch of products.
- A few years later, the entire operations were relocated to another city.
- This was followed shortly thereafter by a merger with a similar sized international company.
- The performance of the U.S. Tech Ops organization had deteriorated, and a change management program was initiated.
- The turnaround succeeded in improving Key Performance Indicators and the methodologies introduced in the US were being adopted by other international sites.
- The head of US Tech Ops moved to Headquarters in Europe to lead the transformation of Tech Ops in other countries.
- Several of my colleagues, who had led various aspects of the change program and implementation were sent to help other

sites establish aspects of the program or became Site Heads in other countries.

- There were two Blacks in US Tech Ops and neither of us was invited to headquarters or other countries to facilitate the transfer of the new approaches.
- Neither of the two of us became Site Heads or assumed a global role of any sort.
- I asked my boss why I had not been given an opportunity even to present the work that I had led, to the leaders in Headquarters.
- His response was either that I should be patient, or that there was a hiring freeze, or that I was needed to build the North American organization.
- After 20 years in the company, I finally got to visit Headquarters to report on a project.
- I grew tired of colleagues saying to me: "we know you are next up for Site Head", and it not occurring.
- The final straw was my being reassigned to report to a former subordinate.
- I decided to interview with other international companies.
- I received an offer to join another company and lead a similar change process in their Tech Ops global organization.
- The base compensation was considerably greater than what I was receiving, and the bonuses, including the retention bonus were considerably greater.
- I informed my boss of the offer and the following day I received a counter offer from the HR department.
- HR also said that they 'were thinking about me' with respect to spending time at Headquarters.
- I decided that the other company had demonstrated their appreciation for my expertise and proven leadership, and therefore accepted their offer.

ENVIRONMENT:

- The company was centralized. All major strategic and product decisions had to be approved by leaders in Headquarters.

- The leaders in Headquarters were treated as though they were the mythical Oracles in Delphi.
- The future leaders in Headquarters were given assignments in the US and other major countries.
- Rising stars in the US were given exposure, either by being assigned to international projects or to short-term management assignments at Headquarters.
- Some have been appointed Site Heads of appropriate major departments in countries outside of the US.
- Although the workforce in the US was somewhat diverse, in other countries the employees and middle/upper-level managers reflected the culture and ethnicity of the country except at the highest levels.
- The highest-level positions were often occupied by leaders from Headquarters.

PROBLEM STATEMENT:

- There was a lack of transparency of the selection process and identification of the specific hurdles that needed to be overcome in order to be selected for a Site Head role.

ISSUES SURROUNDING INCLUSION:

Microassaults:

- VM was made to report to a former subordinate.
- The alacrity with which his company produced a counteroffer is most troubling and suggests that VM was being abused.

Microinsults:

- No **microinsults** were reported.

Microinvalidations:

- There were frequent requests for him to be patient while his peers were being rewarded with assignments at Headquarters and other overseas sites.

- Despite exemplary performance reviews for 20 years, he never received an explanation as to why he was never selected to present or work at Headquarters in Europe.
- Although recognized as one of the drivers of the very successful Change Management and Transformation Program of the North American Technical Operations, VM was not rewarded with presentations at Headquarters, nor with being asked to help other countries implement the new approaches.

ISSUES SURROUNDING EQUITY:

Privilege/Preferences:

- White males who received extra assignments that allowed interactions with Headquarters seemed to be on a fast track.

Processes:

- Hierarchical structure inhibited VM approaching senior management.
- The hierarchical structure also limited the degree to which VM's supervisor could advocate for his receiving an assignment at Headquarters.
- There was little transparency in the promotion-processes for senior management positions.
- There was no transparency regarding the overall evaluation process.
- There was no transparency regarding the criteria used to select candidates for assignments at Headquarters.

Prospects:

- VM's prospects seemed to be limited as he was not assigned a mentor.
- There was no clear explanation as to why he was not even chosen initially to make a presentation at Headquarters.
- The request for him to 'be patient' as the only and consistent response to his inquiries about a position in Headquarters was not promising.

- The selection of his colleagues whose performance evaluations, as far as he knew, were similar to his was not a good omen.
- There were few Blacks in the company and none in high management positions throughout the company.

EQUITY-INCLUSION CULTURE MATRIX

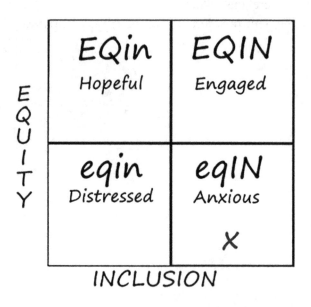

There are two Equity – Inclusion Culture Matrices, one for Headquarters, and one for the US organization. However, although, many major strategic decisions were made by Headquarters, the U.S. organization was responsible for offering the recommendations. This was certainly the case in selection of candidates for an assignment at Headquarters. In the U.S., Privileged individuals were a recognized feature, selection processes were not transparent and VM's prospects, with respect to assignments outside of the U.S. seemed low. He was in a low Equity environment.

At the departmental level, his expertise was recognized and validated in that he was chosen as one of the leaders of the Change Management Transformation Program. He had a supportive manager and advocate. When considering primarily a U.S. Equity-Inclusion Culture Matrix, he is in an **AeqIN- Psychologically Unsafe Culture**. He is anxious, because, in spite of the supportive inclusive actions of his manager and peers, HR and other leaders did not treat him equitably. It was most revealing, that 24 hours after receiving an offer from another company, HR came forward with a counteroffer. This suggests that there was no commitment to making him an Engaged Individual.

When the company promoted one of VM's subordinates to be his boss, the company had moved VM from **AeqIN** to **Deqin**, namely from a **Psychologically Unsafe Cultur**e to a **Psychologically Toxic Culture**.

VM did not have Loss of Voice at the first level. In effect, however, he had no ally that truly spoke on his behalf, and ultimately, there was no organizational process that could or would deal with his issue. Finally, he exercised a 'Hopeful Plan to Endure the Pain'.

A BETTER PROBLEM TO SOLVE:

VM's patience was remarkable. It is surprising that his supervisor and / or HR did not simply tell him that getting an assignment in Headquarters was difficult, but there were opportunities within the US organization. The fact that he started in Quality Assurance, which was in a different department, suggests such opportunities might have existed.

VM's Desired Outcome to become a Site Head for Tech Operations in a major company outside of the U.S. was probably unrealistic. These decisions were made by Headquarters. Consequently, he had no control over the timeframe for this decision. There was also no transparency either about how recommendations in the U.S. were made or how the final selection was determined by Headquarters. Since VM is presently in an **AeqIN Psychologically Unsafe Culture**, his focus should be Inclusion.

VM was validated by being praised for his leadership of the Transformation Process. His Manager was very supportive of him, but had little influence on decisions involving Headquarters. VM also had excellent collaborative relationships with his colleagues. Given the recognition of his achievements in transforming the North American Technical Operations, VM should have considered transferring to positions where his leadership skills could have been used. VM should have engaged his mentor and HR department in the search for a challenging position with more responsibilities. This would have been an opportunity for senior management in the US to address some of the issues of Equity. A focus could be on the Prospects for excellent performers in the organization, who would not be assigned to Headquarters or other countries.

THE REFRAMED PROBLEM:

VM should have engaged his supervisor to approach HR to develop and present to upper management a program to identify opportunities for top performers. This would have helped the organization think more innovatively about this set of employees and the further career development of excellent performers who might be at the pinnacle of their departments. This would improve the retention of these high performers.

This should have been the recommended course before the final **microinsult** and **microinvalidation** of having him report to a subordinate. The Reframed Problem became the one that he solved, namely, securing a similar or better position in a company that valued his contributions and wanted him to be an Engaged Individual.

SYSTEMIC DISCRIMINATION: CASE STUDY # 15 – RW

DESIRED OUTCOME:

- Get my manager to develop interpersonal skills and stop talking down to me.
- Be able to endure my manager's behavior until I can get transfer and promotion to another area of the company.

SITUATION:

- I work for a multi-million dollar telecommunications company with over 10,000 employees.
- I am a Black female who has worked for the company for two years.
- The company has an active Equity, Equality, Diversity and Inclusion (EEDI) program in place.
- There are several White females in senior management but only two Blacks.
- My manager is a rising star and has the ear of senior management.
- Most of the senior management team, including the President and VP, know my name because my manager consistently brags about me in the management meetings.
- I am the first hire my Manager has made in her new position.
- I get excellent reviews and bonuses because I do great work, and she likes me.
- My Manager lacks people skills. She consistently talks down to me and barks out orders when she gives me an assignment.
- Her directions aren't always clear, and she gets upset when one asks for clarification.

- I have addressed the issue with her. She apologizes and says she didn't realize she was being rude; or that she was having a bad day and won't do it again. After a week, she is right back to her old ways.
- Whenever she talks down to me, she will follow it up with an email telling me how awesome I am, and that she just finished telling the senior management team what a great job I am doing.
- She is very controlling and needs to have her ego stroked.
- She constantly praises me to management because it makes her look good.
- I like her as a person and appreciate how she brags about me to management, but I resent the way she talks to me.
- There are ten people on her team, and she talks down to all of us.
- Everyone on the team is afraid to say something because we think she is very vindictive.
- She has attended two mandatory management training courses. She didn't understand why she needed to go to the second training course because she thought that she was already a great manager.
- When she completed the training, the team had to give "anonymous feedback" on any areas she needed to improve.
- She was very annoyed with the team that she didn't receive a perfect rating. How does she grow when she thinks she is perfect?

ENVIRONMENT:

- The size of the staff is over 10,000 employees.
- The percentage of Black employees is less than 1%.
- There are two African Americans in upper management.
- The percentage of White females in upper management is 20%.
- HR is more focused on protecting the company than on developing the employees.

- There is an active EEDI program. My manager is one of the Board members and nominated me to sit on the Board last month.
- I have about 10 years before retirement and am afraid I might lose my job if I make waves.

PROBLEM STATEMENT:

- The manager does not have any interpersonal skills. She needs to develop her people skills. I don't know how much longer I can tolerate her behavior.

ISSUES SURROUNDING INCLUSION:

Microassaults:

- There were no **microassaults** directed solely at RW.
- Every individual in this work unit was addressed in a demeaning manner.

Microinsults:

- Every subordinate was treated as being less worthy of civility than the manager.

Microinvalidations:

- All subordinates were treated in a manner that did not respect their competence.
- Individuals were probably not encouraged to be their authentic selves.

ISSUES SURROUNDING EQUITY:

Privilege/Preferences:

- There was no clear evidence of Privileged groups in the company. There was a suggestion that high performers were recognized. RW described her Manager as a 'rising star' and her having the ear of senior management.

- RW saw great benefit that her Manager often praised her performance during senior management meetings.

Processes:

- It is not easy to engage HR or senior management in resolving difficult management issues.
- There seems to be Fear of Reprisals from a vindictive manager.
- Presence of an 'active' EEDI program does not appear to have increased the number of women in upper management or the number of Blacks in the organization.

Prospects:

- The fear of reprisals from a vindictive manager seemed to determine one's prospects.

EQUITY – INCLUSION CULTURE MATRIX:

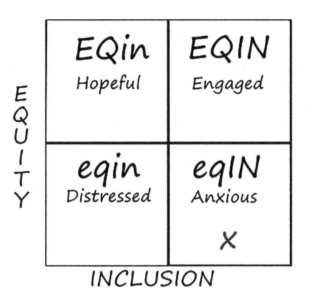

RW and her peers apparently practice Inclusion behaviors and there is respect for each other's contributions in the group. Unfortunately, the poor people management skills of the manager are dampening Individual Engagement and will reduce productivity of the group. RW is not constrained in the area of Inclusion.

Equity presents several problems for RW. Senior management is probably aware of the deficits of RW's manager because they offered her a promotion to a Director position, which had less people responsibility. Her manager declined the promotion. Senior management is treating RW as though she is 'Privileged'. Senior management has also not stepped in to improve the situation in this unit, and the fact that RW and her peers fear retribution from the manager suggests that a vindictive manager can ruin the Prospects of the individual.

RW is in an **AeqIN- Psychologically Unsafe Culture**. She remains anxious because she fears that senior management will do little to improve Equity in her group because of their commitment to the manager. In addition, although RW has an HPEP – Hopeful Plan to Endure the Pain, she fears that her manager could upend the Plan before she can achieve it.

A BETTER PROBLEM TO SOLVE:

RW's Desired Outcome has two components. The first is her manager acquiring better people skills and the second is her getting a transfer with a promotion to another unit. The likelihood that her manager will achieve better people skills in a short time frame is probably not realistic. What would be more realistic is senior management reassigning the manager, but the timeframe for this is also unpredictable. The pursuit of this Outcome would benefit the entire unit and improve Individual Engagement.

The second Outcome is a transfer with a promotion. This Outcome would not necessarily benefit the other members of the group, nor increase the productivity of the unit, but might be achieved in a realistic timeframe. How could RW influence this Outcome?

Both RW and representatives of the group had discussed the manager's problematic style directly with the manager. Unfortunately, both suffered Loss of Voice because they felt that the manager was vindictive. However, the manager has increased RW's Voice in the company by nominating her to become a member of the Board of EEDI. This presents an opportunity for RW to engage her manager in something that is of mutual interest.

A Better Problem to Solve would be getting her manager to sponsor discussions on improving Employee Engagement as part of EEDI activity. Since the manager is a 'Rising Star' and EEDI is viewed positively by senior management, the opportunity to give it practical visibility, by focusing on improving Employee Engagement, has potential. Its impact could be company-wide and this contribution could create opportunities for both a promotion and a transfer for RW.

THE REFRAMED PROBLEM:

The Reframed Problem is finding a way to recruit the manager to work with RW to sponsor an EEDI Employee Engagement Campaign. RW should reach out to HR to help in organizing this Campaign. RW should encourage EEDI to look at the GALLUP data and the Employee Engagement Questionnaire. RW and her Manager should also present what similar sized companies are doing and achieving in their EEDI efforts. This collaboration would also give RW several opportunities to quietly coach her manager in ways to address her subordinates. This Reframe transforms RW from Victim to Mistress of her Fate (a la William Ernest Henley).

SYSTEMIC DISCRIMINATION: CASE STUDY # 16 – LR

DESIRED OUTCOME:

- Make the DEI Steering Committee accept my leadership of DEI.

SITUATION:

- My name is LR and I am a 36-year-old White-passing, straight-looking gay Hispanic female.
- I am an Assistant Project Manager in my company.
- I am well-known for being concerned about the treatment of minorities in our society.
- Following George Floyd's murder, several company-wide discussions were held at my company.
- The CEO agreed to establish a DEI program and tasked the SVP of Legal and Government Affairs with establishing the effort.
- Shortly thereafter, I was called to SVP's office.
- She informed me that the CEO was committed to establishing the DEI program and was anxious to see progress.
- A DEI Steering Committee had been established to support the establishment of the program.
- I had come to the attention of the SVP as I had led two projects in her departments and she was impressed with my performance.
- SVP indicated that she had received approval to appoint me as Leader of the DEI program.
- I was to be initially promoted to Manager and would be reporting directly to the SVP.

- It has been 3 months since my appointment, and I am frustrated with the lack of progress.
- Members of the Steering Committee do not treat me with respect – I am treated as though I am the Committee's secretary.
- The Head of Human Resources (HR) has expressed disagreement with placement of the DEI program under Legal and Government Affairs and not under Human Resources (HR).
- I have not been given resources to help develop the program.
- I feel that I have been set up for failure.
- Some Directors have complained about my accent.
- I am considering resigning from my position.

ENVIRONMENT:

- My company is a midsized American company in the product services and distribution business.
- The Leaders are primarily White males with about 5 % females.
- The general workforce is about 40 % Blacks and Hispanics and about 60% women.
- The SVP is known for having an open-door policy and for treating her direct reports fairly.
- HR department is quite active in trying to resolve employee issues with management, when they occur.
- People are generally cordial with each other, but there is a recognized hierarchy of departments. Those departments that historically bring in the greater revenue have the greater influence.
- There are occasional cross-department workshops to encourage collaboration and improve productivity.
- Project Management is an internal service department within the company.
- There are few Blacks and Hispanics at the Director Level and none at the SVP level.
- The turnover of Blacks and Hispanics is greater than that of Whites.

- There have been occasional attempts to recruit from colleges and universities with high numbers of Black and Hispanic students.

PROBLEM STATEMENT:

- The Director of the Steering Committee does not accept my being appointed to this position because I am Hispanic.

ISSUES SURROUNDING INCLUSION:

Microassaults:

- Some Directors complained about LR's accent.

Microinsults:

- Some Directors complained about LR's accent.

Microinvalidations:

- Lack of resources impaired LR's ability to perform.
- LR felt that the DEI Steering Committee was treating her as though she were secretary to the group.
- LR was not recognized as the leader, although appointed to that position.
- No Goals were established for the Program.

ISSUES SURROUNDING EQUITY:

Privilege/Preferences:

- There are no Hispanics or Blacks at the SVP level.
- There is a small number of Hispanics and Blacks at Director Level.
- Departments producing greater revenues have greater influence.
- Although 60% of employees were female, only 5% of the leadership group was female.

Processes:

- The decision-making around leadership positions was not transparent.
- SVP had not adequately prepared LR for her new assignment.

Prospects:

- LR's Prospects seem excellent.
- She had been selected to lead a project involving individuals from two departments and had received positive comments on her performance from the SVP.
- The SVP had recommended her to lead the new DEI effort, reporting directly to the SVP as manager of the DEI Program.
- This is a significant recognition and promotion.

EQUITY – INCLUSION CULTURE MATRIX

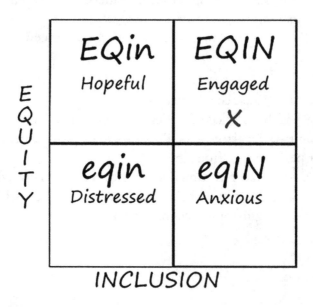

There was clearly a preference for White males in leadership positions. Nonetheless, the female SVP, who was Head of the Legal and Government Affairs Departments, had the respect of the CEO in that she was charged with establishing the new DEI Program. This program was approved by the CEO and, as a result, had great visibility. Thus, the CEO was demonstrating his commitment by establishing the DEI program in the company.

The fact that the HR department was actively involved in resolving employee issues with management also suggests a culture where fairness was important. In addition, the Head of HR had expressed his disappointment that HR had not been given the responsibility to develop the DEI program, which suggests that he was committed to DEI.

LR describes a general cordial environment and the SVP as an approachable leader who was supportive of her direct reports.

Although there were no targeted DEI programs in existence, there seemed to be general alignment with DEI. This was evidenced by the apparent desires of the CEO to have an equitable culture, as well as by the personal efforts of the SVP to promote Inclusion behaviors. LR is presently low in the **EEQIN- Psychologically Safe Culture.**

Given that LR was in the **EEQIN-Psychologically Safe Culture** quadrant, during the interview, the VIP panel asked LR whether there was clarity between her responsibilities and the role of the DEI Steering Committee. She responded in the negative. Her response to the question as to whether she had created SMART goals was also negative. The VIP panel concluded that LR was not suffering from Loss of Voice and her establishing a 'Hopeful Plan to Endure the Pain' was premature.

A BETTER PROBLEM TO SOLVE:

LR's Desired Outcome to have the DEI Steering Committee accept her leadership is potentially realistic, even though she believed that this lack of acceptance was because she is Hispanic. LR did not give examples to support this belief. Nonetheless, this problem can be addressed in a realistic time frame.

It will be critical for there to be a Dialogue between LR and the DEI Steering Committee. This Dialogue is also essential to get this new program on a successful path which could provide a realistic benefit to many employees and the company. Thus, a Better Problem to Solve, is one that would facilitate a meaningful Dialogue between LR and the DEI Steering Committee.

THE REFRAMED PROBLEM:

The Reframed Problem is creation of the Dialogue with the DEI Committee to ensure the successful launch of the DEI Program.

The VIP panel recommended that LR create 3-4 SMART goals and seek input and guidance from the Head of HR. Thereafter, LR should discuss the goals with her boss, the SVP, for her input and approval.

Dr. Frank L. Douglas

Once achieved, LR should then ask the SVP to organize a DEI Launch meeting, to present and discuss Mission, SMART Goals, LR's Role, and the Role of the DEI Steering Committee. This meeting must be chaired by the SVP.

SYSTEMIC DISCRIMINATION: CASE STUDY # 17 – EJ

DESIRED OUTCOME:

- To hire an assistant to deal with Programming.

SITUATION:

- My name is EJ and I have a Master's degree in Librarian Sciences.
- I supervised 10 employees for several years, in my capacity as Adult Services Librarian Manager.
- About 10 years ago, I received a promotion to the position of Assistant Branch Manager.
- Shortly after my promotion, a White female was hired as Branch Manager.
- The new hire had a Bachelor's degree and little experience in Library Services Management.
- The Job of Branch Manager encompassed multiple responsibilities including supervision of staff, budget management and strategic projects.
- Since my new boss had no knowledge or experience in performing the aforementioned tasks, she delegated them to me.
- Part of the delegated tasks included Programming which was time-consuming and usually had a dedicated person assigned to that area.
- I liked my job because the extended responsibilities increased my social and business networks.
- My boss gave me excellent reviews and knew that without me the branch could not function.

- I retired at the age of 62 and started my own consultant business where I am in great demand.

ENVIRONMENT:

- The staff consisted of 50-60 employees.
- 15% of the staff consisted of Black and Hispanic employees.
- The Director of the Library was Black but primarily did what the White staff wanted.
- Human Resources was relatively helpful, but there were few problems.

PROBLEM STATEMENT:

- The selection process was not transparent or based on academic and work experience in Library Sciences.

ISSUES SURROUNDING INCLUSION:

Microassaults:

- No **microassaults** were reported.

Microinsults:

- No **microinsults** were reported.

Microinvalidations:

- A White female with a B.S. was appointed as Branch Manager and EJ's Boss. EJ had an M.S. and more experience in management of Library Services.
- EJ was not provided a manager of programming, so she had a greater workload.

ISSUES SURROUNDING EQUITY:

Privilege/Preferences:

- The Director of the Library, although Black, catered to the White employees.

- A White female with less academic qualifications and experience was appointed Manager of Library Services and EJ's boss.

Processes:

- The Black Director of the Library catered to the White employees.

Prospects:

- The only possibility for advancement for EJ was her boss' job.

EQUITY – INCLUSION CULTURE MATRIX:

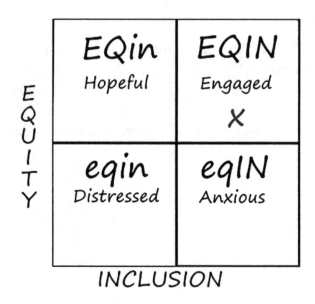

Apart from a clear Preference for and the processes that support White employees, EJ was generally not oppressed by the lack of full Equity. With respect to Inclusion, her expertise was appreciated by her boss who delegated many tasks to her. Her boss also further affirmed her by giving her excellent evaluations for her performance. EJ is actually in an **EEQIN-Psychologically Safe Culture** and her own Engagement was based on her identifying and exploiting the best possibilities of her reality. EJ had a 'Hopeful Plan to Endure the Pain'. She was 2-3 years away from retirement and found that her present situation was providing significant social and professional networks that could be useful in her subsequent life as a consultant. As a result, Loss of Voice was not important to her.

A BETTER PROBLEM TO SOLVE:

EJ's Desired Outcome was to receive an assistant to deal with programming tasks. Assuming the budget was available, recruiting an assistant to manage programming could be achieved in a realistic timeframe. The various people being supported by the programming function would benefit from the hire of an assistant to manage programing, and EJ's engagement and productivity would improve. Given the relatively cordial relationship between the White female boss and EJ, it would have made sense for EJ to repeat her request more forcefully for the programming assistant. EJ could have solicited memos from her library clients as part of her documentation of the need for a programming assistant.

THE REFRAMED PROBLEM:

EJ was still upset about having been passed over and consequently wanted transparency regarding the criteria used in appointing Branch Managers. EJ could have narrowed her problem to requesting a review of processes for hiring assistant managers and could have asked her boss to help in this endeavor.

However, EJ did not Reframe the Problem. She **Reframed her Experience**. EJ recognized that her present position was increasing both her social and professional networks. Since she was two to three years away from her planned retirement, she decided to leverage the present position to build those networks which could be very helpful in her post-retirement life as a consultant.

SYSTEMIC DISCRIMINATION: CASE STUDY # 18 – EM

DESIRED OUTCOME:

- I would like to move to a different part of the organization.

SITUATION:

- On completing my Bachelor of Science Degree in Mathematics, with a minor in Physics, I obtained a job as a math analyst for a major corporation.
- I was one of the very few African Americans employed there.
- I was excited about entering the workforce and eager to apply mathematics to real life situations. I gave up an opportunity for a free ride to graduate school at Carnegie Mellon University for mathematics, so, I knew this job had to work.
- About six months later I received a call from Human Resources (HR) asking if I would be interested in a position in compensation and benefits.
- They needed someone with my skills to complete a programming project.
- All went well and I enjoyed working with the new team and my boss was an absolutely wonderful person to work for.
- My work world euphoria came to a halt when my boss decided to move to Arizona to be with her daughter's family.
- Her replacement was an older gentleman from Alabama.
- My world changed drastically.
- My new manager always found fault with my work. Either the reports did not address the assignment or there were not enough studies reviewed.

- When I questioned his logic, he would become flustered and often remarked that he was the boss and that was the only thing that counted.
- During departmental meetings, I would raise my hand to be recognized and he would ignore me. It was only when one of my White colleagues pointed out that my hand was raised, he would respond.
- Often, he was rude and would interrupt me and infer that my contribution was stupid or not worth answering.
- My colleagues recognized how he treated me and remarked quietly that they thought he was wrong, and that I should complain.
- I had no intention of complaining to the Vice President of Human Resources, who was also an African American because I had a plan. At the first opportunity, I planned to transfer to another department.
- During meetings, my boss had certain "go-to" persons from whom he sought information, with whom he joked, whose affirmation he sought, and then there was I.
- At one point I was given an assignment by the Vice President of Human Resources (VP) to develop a new benefits package for employees that would not result in a corporate cost increase.
- I set to work studying the level of benefits employees were provided and degree of usage. I developed a package deal that resulted in incentives for college reimbursements and carpooling benefits, and redesigned the benefits package to be more attractive and user-friendly.
- Upon completion, I submitted the package directly to the VP, who was very pleased with it, and forwarded it to the corporate President to be considered for implementation.
- The next day my boss called me into his office and reprimanded me severely that I had not informed him that the project was completed.
- I was informed never to send any assignment out of the office without his permission or else there would be consequences.

- I found it interesting that I was given an assignment directly from the VP which my boss knew nothing about.
- Once a meeting was called by the VP and I was not sent a notice regarding the meeting.
- However, because I had spoken to the VP earlier that morning, he asked my boss why I was not present.
- My friends told me that my boss had responded that he didn't know.
- The VP called me directly from the meeting and asked that I join them. Upon my arrival I announced an apology and indicated that I was not made aware of the meeting.
- By this time, I had worked for my boss for about eight months, and I was tired of his racist behavior.
- My colleagues received outstanding ratings while I was receiving satisfactory ratings.
- Requests for days off were denied because he did not want too many persons out of the office at the same time.
- I rarely requested time off and yet I watched as others arrived late or called in sick. Later, they would arrive the next day and discuss what they had really done on their sick day off.
- It was at this point that I started to study the behavior of my boss. In meetings with the VP of HR I observed the cynical expressions he would make when the VP was talking.
- During meetings, my boss often commented that operations ran more smoothly in the place where he had previously worked compared to the present company.
- Once when he remarked about the better operations at his former place of employment, the VP commented that he might consider going back. That led to a few snickers around the table. My boss turned as red as a beet and ceased making negative comments.
- On another occasion my boss was on vacation, and I received a call from the President of the corporation for a meeting. I was asked to develop an executive employee benefits package for an incoming President of the twin corporation, and it should be commensurate with his position.

- I assembled a benefits package that mirrored the employee package with the exception of the pension benefits plan. Such benefits are closely regulated by the Pension Benefits Guarantee Fund and so I recommended purchasing an independent policy offering executive-level pension benefits.
- My decision was supported by legal documentation and industry trends data.
- My proposal was accepted as sound by the legal department and the President of the corporation.
- Needless to say, when my boss returned to work and heard about my proposal to the President, he was furious. I tried to explain to him that the report was needed that day. He didn't care.
- At this point when I left my boss' office I went directly to the VP of HR and informed him of what had occurred. He told me he would handle it. This event occurred on a Thursday, and I was off on Friday.
- When I returned to work on Monday, everyone was asking what had happened between myself and the boss. They had heard everything he said to me in the office on Thursday because he was shouting.
- I was informed that on Friday when my boss arrived, he was asked to go directly to the President's office.
- He returned to the office with his head hanging low and went directly to his office and closed the door. His door opened shortly thereafter and he departed carrying a box in his hands.
- He had been fired. It was never discussed why he was fired.
- Although my experience was unpleasant, I learned an invaluable lesson. In the words of Dale Renton, "when what you hear and what you see don't match, trust your eyes."
- I learned to focus on human behavior, observing words and actions. I left the corporate scene to return to school to obtain a law degree.

ENVIRONMENT:

- The company had about 2500 employees with about 20 % being minorities.
- The focus of the company was administration of insurance claims.
- The Vice President of HR was the only Black (a male) among the Directors and Vice Presidents.
- There was a large HR department about 40 employees, of which 5 were Black.
- Because of my skills in programming, and particularly my knowledge of Fortran, I was assigned special projects to support HR. This included assessment of the competitiveness of the company's Benefit Packages and recommendations of additional, creative benefits that would distinguish the company.
- My first boss, a White Female, was very supportive and had created a very positive environment.
- Her replacement was a White male, who from our first interaction seemed to have a not so veiled dislike of me.
- This dislike was evidenced in several ways. He would ignore me when I raised my hand to make a comment. This was so obvious that on occasion, guests attending the meeting had prefaced their own comments by remarking that they would make their own comment after I had had an opportunity to make mine.
- During weekly reports, whereas other colleagues would receive encouraging comments and praise for their progress, my reports were met with criticism.
- My attempts to meet with him to discuss my projects were either frustrated, or were brief and not helpful.

PROBLEM STATEMENT:

- This manger seemed to have an uncontrolled hostility towards Black females.

ISSUES SURROUNDING INCLUSION:

Microassaults:

- EM's new boss was hypercritical of everything she did.
- He asserted his position as the boss when confronted with his inconsistencies.
- EM was rebuked by her immediate boss for completing and submitting a project that was assigned by the VP of Human Resources.
- EM's new boss was openly hostile and condescending.
- He ignored EM's raised hand in meetings, unless prompted by other colleagues.
- During meetings, EM was subject to frequent interruptions from her boss.

Microinsults:

- EM experienced looks of disdain from her new boss.

Microinvalidations:

- EM's new boss ignored her during staff meetings unless called out by her White colleagues.
- He constantly interrupted EM while she was speaking.
- EM was not rewarded consistent with the quality of the work she was producing.
- The new boss excluded EM from a meeting which the VP had organized and then was less than truthful as to why she was not present.
- The new boss was openly angry/hostile that EM was being recognized by the VP and the corporate CEO.

ISSUES SURROUNDING EQUITY:

Privilege/Preferences:

- EM's boss had a group of favored subordinates with whom he interacted and socialized.

- He denied paid time off for EM while her White colleagues were allowed to arrive late, call in sick or have time off without recrimination.

Processes:

- It was unclear if there was a process in place for arbitration of this unusual situation.
- EM decided early on not to go to HR about the experiences she was encountering.
- There is a question about the process that led to the hiring of this particular boss whose values seemed to be at odds with that of the organization.

Prospects:

- EM's prospects in this organization went from good to poor to excellent – her initial boss was fully supportive of her. That boss's replacement treated her with a great deal of hostility, but his superiors were extremely supportive and recognized her value.

EQUITY-INCLUSION CULTURE MATRIX:

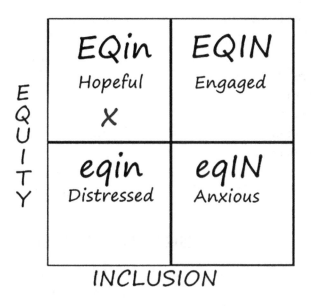

EM's initial boss was supportive of her work and she scored high on both Equity and Inclusion, placing her in **EEQIN** category – that of a highly motivated and engaged employee. However, her initial boss's replacement was openly hostile and devalued her at every opportunity and in effect, created a toxic work environment. She then dropped from **EEQIN** in the Equity-Inclusion Culture Matrix to **Deqin** – a distressed employee. In this situation EM clearly had Loss of Voice at the First and Second levels, in that she was afraid to complain about the treatment from her boss and there seemed to be no colleague, who would serve as an ally and confront her boss on her behalf. Her colleagues, however, let her know that they were aware of the awful way she was being treated by their new boss.

It is unclear why EM chose not to discuss her problems with the VP of Human Resources. However, when she finally was requested by the VP of HR to explain what had occurred with her boss, a definitive action, namely his termination from the company, was the immediate consequence. So, there was no Loss of Voice at the organization level.

EM's recognition by the VP and Corporate CEO moved her from **Deqin** to **HEQin** – hopeful, which allowed her to focus on her tasks and remain optimistic about her plan to go to Law School. This ultimately replaced her 'Hopeful Plan to Endure the Pain' of working under this supervisor. Initially, that plan was to seek a transfer to another department. This case is quite instructive in demonstrating the role of senior management in establishing Equity and the role of frontline managers in encouraging behaviors that foster Inclusion. It also demonstrates how an Individual could go from working in an **EEQIN** culture to a **Deqin** Culture through the replacement of a single manager!

A BETTER PROBLEM TO SOLVE:

EM clearly had strong, practical, albeit silent support with respect to Equity, in that she was strongly validated by the CEO and the VP of Human Resources. As a result, her Desired Outcome to transfer to another department was probably quite realistic both in terms of timeframe and success.

EM's problem lay with respect to her being denied Inclusion by her supervisor. This was also observed by her colleagues as well as a visitor in one of the meetings. EM could have focused on the productivity of the meeting process. She could have identified potential colleagues as allies and asked them to discuss openly, the need for rules of conduct for meetings to ensure that everyone is engaged, and the best ideas are brought forward. This approach could be achieved in a short timeframe and would have facilitated a realistic dialogue with the Supervisor and this could have benefited all participants.

If EM could not find allies to achieve this approach, she could then have sought advice from the VP of HR on ways to improve discussion and sharing of ideas in her department.

THE REFRAMED PROBLEM:

The Reframed Problem would be how to achieve Inclusion. Since EM clearly had the support of the VP of HR, and the CEO of the organization, this was a realistic achievement from which all would have benefitted.

CLOSING THOUGHTS

I would like to thank the many interviewees who not only were generous with their time during the interview process but were helpful in reviewing the SHD Reframe Intake Form for accuracy. I would also again like to thank our Victors over Injustice in their Professions (VIPs) for the engaged discussions as we used the SHD Reframing Process to find A Better Problem to Solve. Our VIPs have been acknowledged at the beginning of this Primer.

The SHD Reframing Process uncovered a number of issues that are worthy of mention as we consider the real-world impact of Systemic Discrimination. All but two interviewees (EJ and EM) expressed that they were reliving PTSD-like symptoms as they recounted their experiences. It is important that leaders of organizations consider that a Psychologically Toxic Culture, that is a culture with low Equity and low Inclusion, might be causing significant emotional harm to their employees. This harm, which I coin under the phrase, 'Organizational Cultural Stress Disorder', we believe, is often unrecognized and underestimated. Besides its impact on individuals, it may also have significant negative consequences for engagement, productivity and profitability.

The Diagnostic and Statistical Manual of Mental Disorders (DSM-5) asserts that the response to trauma or a stressor may manifest as general unhappiness with life, anger and aggression, or disengagement/detachment from life experiences (4). In addition, Dr. Monica Williams has raised the alarm that, as identified in these cases, subtle, continuous racism could have PTSD-like effects similar to those that can occur from a major traumatic racist event (5). We believe that PTSD-like effects occur in those affected by the George Floyd murder and that OCSD effects occur in a number of the cases presented in this primer. More investigation is needed to characterize and differentiate the effects due to a single, horrific racist event from those due to continual **microaggressions** and inequities.

Secondly, we have found that although an organization may generally have a Psychologically Safe Culture, there may be **Individuals** who are experiencing a Psychologically Unsafe subculture within the organization. This fact reinforces the importance of SHD's focus on the individual.

Thirdly, it is our belief that a **Deqin** individual, that is a Distressed Individual in a low equity, low inclusion culture, might still find ways to improve their situation by using the SHD Reframing Process. This is possible because the goal is to empower the Affected Individual to find solutions that increase their engagement.

These cases also illustrate that senior leaders are responsible for establishing Equity in the organization, and frontline managers and coworkers are responsible for fostering the behaviors that sustain Inclusion. When Equity and Inclusion do not support each other, Psychologically Unsafe Cultures develop.

Finally, Loss of Voice may adversely affect Individual Engagement leading to loss of personal and organizational productivity.

Loss of Voice can occur at any of three levels. Loss of Voice at the First Level occurs when the affected individual is inhibited from discussing the discrimination that they are experiencing. With Loss of Voice at the Second Level, there are no allies available or willing to support the affected individual. Loss of Voice at the Third Level occurs when there are no effective, official organizational advocates to address employee or member complaints without there being fear of reprisals.

We recognize that these observations have been made on a small number of cases. However, for each interviewee, the experience of Systemic Discrimination was real, unforgettable, and impactful.

REFERENCES AND SOURCES

1) SHRM Report: The Journey of Equity & Inclusion, Summer, 2020
2) Harter JK, et. al. The Relationship Between Engagement at Work and Organizational Outcomes Gallup 2020 Q12 Meta-analysis, 10th/edition
3) Agrawal S., Harter JK, Employee Engagement Influences Involvement in Wellness Programs, 2009, Gallup
4) Diagnostic and Statistical Manual of Mental Disorders, 5th Edition
5) Williams, M. T., Osman, M., Gran-Ruaz, S., & Lopez, J. (2021). Intersection of racism and PTSD: Assessment and treatment of racism-related stress and trauma. *Current Treatment Options in Psychiatry 8. 167-185*

GLOSSARY

A	Anxious
D	Distressed
E	Engaged
H	Hopeful
EQ	Equity
IN	Inclusion
eq	low equity
in	low inclusion
EQIN	High Equity, High Inclusion
EQin	High Equity, low inclusion
eqIN	low equity, High Inclusion
eqin	low equity, low inclusion
AeqIN	low equity, High Inclusion culture with anxious individuals
Deqin	low equity, low inclusion culture with distressed individuals
EEQIN	High Equity, High Inclusion culture, with engaged individuals
HEQin	High Equity, low inclusion culture, with hopeful individuals
HPEP	Hopeful Plan to Endure the Pain

CPSIA information can be obtained
at www.ICGtesting.com
Printed in the USA
LVHW021935120423
744168LV00001B/218